"If you want to be successful, find someone who has achieved the results you want and copy what they do and you'll achieve the same results."
Tony Robbins

"Tom Monson earned millions as an award-winning author, filmmaker, and director, and he did all those things because he is a sales giant." Lane Shultz

"Written in simple layman's terms this book is easy to understand, well written and organized in such a way that it takes the reader step by step to the conclusion -- Successful Selling. This book should be in every businessperson's library." Shirley Roe of Allbooks Reviews

"If you are in any sales career, even if it is just to 'sell yourself,' this book could revolutionize the entire outcome of your life. Highly Recommended." Janet Elaine Smith, MyShelf.com

Sales Giant

How to master the art of selling in just 90 days

By Thomas N. Monson

Sales Giant , Fourth Edition
Originally Published as
You Gotta Wanna, Traits of the Sales Greats
Copyright 2004 - 2020 by Thomas Nash Monson
All rights reserved.

Library of Congress Cataloging-in-Publication Data

Monson, Thomas N., 1948 -

HF5438.25.K343 2004
658.85--dc22
2004012385

ISBN 978-0-570-73990-0

Sales Giant

How to master the art of selling in just 90 days

By Thomas N. Monson

Successful Selling

Becoming A Sales Giant

Introduction

Welcome to your journey to become a *Sales Giant*!

Journey?

Yes, this is a journey and I'll show you how to get there. I'll tell you what you need to do and what you need to know to sell more of your products or services.

It's your journey and your success is in your hands. All I can do is show you the way. You have to do all the hard work.

In my first 50 years of sales, I've discovered that there are at least 62 principles needed to achieve sales excellence. Now they belong to you. If you use them, they will take you to the next level.

How Far do You Want to Go?

What is your next level? If you are not already there, your first goal should be to break into the top 20% of salespeople because they are earning 80% of all the commissions paid.

If you're already in the top 20%, you realize there is still much to learn. Maybe I can help organize your talents, knowledge, and understanding of sales, and who knows, possibly fill in a few knowledge gaps.

Can You be Successful?

First, you have to realize you are an individual like no other individual who has walked the face of our planet. You have every right to be successful. There is no profile for success except for one's level of desire.

How Can You Get the Most from this Book?

Principle six is about goals and how they are an important part of your success. You should have goals for learning the contents of this book.

I suggest you read the book cover to cover because most of these principles are inner-related. Let me give you an example, if you properly qualify a prospect, make a powerful presentation, notice positive body language, and hear buying signals, then closing this sale will be a very natural event. By first reading this book all the way through, you will see the connections.

After reading the entire book, study it section by section, do the exercises, and check your answers with the answers provided. This book was designed to help you deeply learn these principles so you can benefit at the highest possible level.

I've divided the book into four sections.

The Basics of Success

In this section, I have put together a collection of principles you will want to follow to be successful at anything you do. Even if you're not in sales, these principles have been used by almost every successful person.

Prospects and Prospecting

What is the life blood of any business? This section contains several ways to attract, acquire, organize, and qualify your prospective customers or clients.

The Selling Process

Can you increase your sales to presentation success rate? Selling isn't rocket science. If you do it right, you can become rich. This section contains the fundamental rules that have been used ever since a potter sold a clay pot to a woman in the next village.

Becoming The Sales Giant

What does it take to rise above your competition? It's all about how you deal with your customers, and how you deal with the day to day issues faced by everyone in business.

Bibliography

In the back of the book there is a bibliography to help you identify some great books to help sharpen your skills. You will soon realize the process of becoming *a Sales Giant* will be a consistent and never-ending pursuit of excellence.

Conclusion

Your success is your journey. It will be the result of the work you do and the problems you solve for your customers.

Do I have all the answers?" Of course not, but I promise if you go through this book lesson by lesson, you will be on your way to becoming *a Sales Giant*.

Tom Monson

Basics of Success

1 - Why do You Want to be A Sales Giant?

What one trait do you need to the best you can be?

Every great salesperson has a great desire to be great. Salespeople without desire are like tires without air. They usually don't go very far.

Great salespeople don't push the snooze button. They don't count the days until Friday. They don't watch the clock to see when they can go home. They look forward to each day with unbridled enthusiasm. They see only potential and opportunities. Their passion for success overrides fear, rejection, and obstacles.

Their passion is reflected in what they do and the way they walk, talk, dress, and interact with people. Passion cannot be faked. It is authentic. Salespeople are genuinely proud of their profession. They never think salespeople are pesky and pushy. They recognize that the world needs their product or service, and they are there to fulfill customers' needs.

There are many people who are content just to get by. As long as they get their paycheck, pay the bills, and support their family, they are satisfied to just go along to get along. They never have the need to be great as long as their basic needs are met. Great salespeople want more. They constantly strive to better themselves, their skills, and their relationships with people. They love what they do. They think it is so wonderful that they feel the need to share that love with other people.

Salespeople are so passionate about what they do that they take the steps necessary to get better. They want to learn more. They do research to improve their knowledge and strive to develop their skills. They anticipate the future with eagerness and an open mind. They work at getting better without it seeming like work. They go above and beyond the call of duty, never settling for mediocrity. They never give up.

Finally, salespeople convey this passion to their customers by describing their products and services with vivid images and pictures. They focus on the benefits and not the features. If it's a convertible sports car, they emphasize how it will feel racing down the freeway with the wind whipping through your hair. And, if the customer has to go to the beauty salon after racing down the freeway with the wind whipping through his or her hair, the salesperson tells them how much younger he or she will look and feel with some new blonde highlights.

Salespeople can be spectators or they can be players. Sales is not for everyone. It is only for those who have a genuine, burning desire to identify people's problems and help them find solutions. Salespeople must love people, and they must be one-hundred percent behind their product or service. Only then will people be convinced to buy. Only then will salespeople be happy to get out of bed each morning.

Questions

1. How motivated are you to go to work each day?

2. What would motivate you even more?

3. What are some things that would squelch your passion?

4. Explain the ways you express passion for your profession.

5. How do you feel about the future of your job?

6. Can you honestly say you are in the right line of work? Why or why not?

Answers

1. Time to think about the level of satisfaction with your job. If your job satisfaction is low, it may be time to think about whether you are doing what you really enjoy.

2. Think about what you would like to accomplish in your job. Do you have goals and are they goals you are passionate about?

3. Write down things that interfere with your motivation. What annoys you at work and are there ways you can deal with annoyances?

4. If you were someone else observing you, describe specific behaviors that convey eagerness and passion in your job.

5. Talk about what you look forward to and whether or not you feel your job is going in the right direction. Do you feel excited about the future or is there a feeling of doom and gloom?

6. Think about your character and drive. Are they in line with what it takes to be successful at sales? What about you do you think may not be suitable for the sales profession?

2 - Integrity

What is the most admired trait of the wealthy?

For many years, salespeople have been getting a bad rap because of a few con artists. These crooks lie to their customers to make a sale. They do whatever it takes. A lack of ethics is what allows criminals to fleece their victims.

There is an old saying about how people are the architects of their own character. What people choose, what they think, and what they do, contribute to who they become. If you choose to be dishonest, then that is who you will become. It all starts with the first time you tell a little white lie to a customer.

Salespeople who lie will always lose eventually. They lose in the short run because they do not benefit from the personal growth of making honest sales. Every time you make an honest sale, you build character, confidence, and poise. These are critical elements for future success.

Salespeople who lie lose in the end because they are never able to advance to a higher level. The truth always comes out. Management and customers eventually learn about the lies. This forces con artists to move on or into a different line of work. The path of dishonesty most often ends in poverty and disparity.

The dishonest salespeople never know the freedom found in always telling the truth. They never know the contentment found in honor. They believe that everyone is like them—looking for the easy buck and willing to do anything to make it. They never know the satisfaction found in hard work and trust.

Integrity is not just for salespeople, it is at the core of all successful people. If you want to be successful in your job, your relationships with friends and family, your relationships with your business associates, you have to be a person of high integrity. Integrity is what makes you trustworthy.

Surveys of millionaires show that the number one trait valued by wealthy people is integrity. Think about it, if you had lots of money, would you trust it to someone who has not demonstrated that he or she is trustworthy?

How can you be honest? Live your life as if it were an open book. Think about the consequences of your actions today. Ask yourself, "If I do this today, will I be able to tell my customers and others about it later and still have them trust me?"

For lasting success, you need to be honest with your customers and with yourself. Telling the truth is sometimes hard, but it is always the easiest and most rewarding route to take.

Questions

1. Why do you think integrity is important in business?

2. Why do you think integrity is important in personal relationships?

3. Thinking about a person you admire, name three ways they demonstrate integrity?

a.

b.

c.

4. Name three ways you can demonstrate your personal integrity.

a.

b.

c.

5. How can you protect your integrity if you are around people who do not possess integrity?

Answers

1.   Integrity is the backbone of trust. If you are in business with someone, you have to trust them. They hold the keys to your fortune and your future -- you have to trust them. If you can't trust them, move on and find someone you can.

2.   Guess what? Relationships are built on trust. There is an old saying, if you cheated on them you'll probably cheat on me. The quality of your personal relationship will be in direct proportion to the amount of integrity you posess.

3.   I have always admired Theodore Roosevelt. In his words:

   a."In any moment of decision, the best thing you can do is the right thing. The worst thing you can do is nothing."

   b."The things that will destroy America are prosperity at any price, peace at any price, safety first instead of duty first and love of soft living and the get-rich-quick theory of life."

   c."To educate a person in the mind but not in morals is to educate a menace to society."

4.   Here is how I demonstrate my integrity.

   a. I am always truthful.

   b. When I work with a customer, I always put their needs ahead of all others' -- including my own.

   c. If I tell someone I am going to do something, you can bet I will give it my best to accomplish the task.

5.   You can't. If you want to be happy and wealthy, you have to associate with upstanding people.

3 - Building Trust

How do you build trust?

The most fundamental elements of a lasting relationship with customers is integrity and that manifests itself into trust and reliability. Think about it. Would you rather buy a car from someone all your friends recommend or from someone you know nothing about? You'd probably buy from someone recommended by your friends. Why? Because they all had good experiences and so you feel confident that you will too. And the more recommendations you get, the more confident and trusting you become. People will happily pay for peace of mind.

Studies have shown that the number one reason people choose to buy from a particular vendor is because they trust them. You build that trust by being reliable. Reliable means being dependable, consistent, steadfast, unswerving, unfailing, and trustworthy. It all comes back to trust.

How do you get people to trust you? Trust is earned over time. It is unlikely that prospects will trust you the first time they meet you. They may have a hunch, an inclination, or a sixth sense that you're acceptable, or they might have heard something about you, or be in a hurry to fill a need, or they don't like the alternatives.

You can begin to build trust right from the start. Look at your business through your customer's eyes. What do you trust about yourself? Does what you say instill trust? Do your actions convey reliability? Being reliable is doing what you say you are going to do, doing it on time, and doing it right.

No doubt mistakes will be made sooner or later. When mistakes do occur, they are an opportunity to build trust. Part of a customer's judgment of you will be based on how well you handle problems. Use this opportunity to show you care about your customers and that you provide excellent service. When something goes wrong, let the customer know immediately. Keeping customers informed builds trust. Leaving them in the dark makes them suspicious and uneasy. If they find out about a problem on their own, they may become angry and confrontational and feel you abandoned them.

Follow through. This isn't as easy as it sounds, but it's very important. You need to perform each step that the customer expects and pay attention to the details of every job. Complete a project to the end and you'll let your customer know that persistence and following through are ingrained in your service policy.

Sometimes people want to make a sale so badly they will make unrealistic promises. When they can't deliver, they get a reputation for being unreliable. What you want to do is underpromise and overdeliver. This makes customers think they got a deal, that your service is excellent because they got more than they expected. The ability to keep a promise can define your personality and your business. Think twice before you promise something. Make sure you can keep that promise. If you cannot keep a promise, be honest and forthright. Then make a new promise, but be sure to keep it. Two broken promises could be fatal to a relationship. And never trust your memory. Write down promises, and put them somewhere you will be sure to see them.

Always tell the truth. People who stretch the truth or tell lies will eventually stumble on their own words and be caught. Then they have to tell more lies to straighten out their story. If you are caught in a lie, customers will never trust you again. Why should they?

You should care enough about your customers to take a genuine interest in their needs. This will earn their trust. Do what you say you're going to do and do it on time. Follow through to the end. Avoid mistakes, but when you do make them, use them as opportunities to show your customers how you can fix their problem reliably. Over time, you will strengthen your relationships, and loyalty to your business will grow.

Questions

1. Can you think of a company you do business with because you trust it? What is it about that company makes you trust it?

2. Can you think of a company you don't trust? Why don't you trust it?

3. What does being reliable mean to you?

4. As a customer, how do you respond to businesses that do not seem reliable to you?

5. Can you tell when a customer is skeptical of you? How do you respond?

6. How do you handle mistakes? Do customers seem pleased with how you handle them?

7. How are you at following through? How could you improve at following through?

8. Give an example of a time when you underpromised and overdelivered.

9. Have you ever been caught in a white lie? How did you explain yourself and what was the other person's reaction?

Answers

1. More than likely the company has a reputation for reliability and fairness. You may also be good friends with the owner. Or, it may be that the company hasn't given you a reason not to trust it.

2. Maybe you had a bad experience. Or you know from talking to people that the company has a bad reputation. Or you know from reading the newspaper that the company gets sued often.

3. This question is asking you to define your standards for judging a company as reliable.

4. Do you put up with businesses that seem unreliable because the benefits outweigh the costs? Or do you take your business somewhere else?

5. Describe your plan of action when it seems that a customer doesn't trust you.

6. Describe what you do to correct mistakes and deal with unhappy customers. From your observation, do customers seem pleased with how you handled mistakes?

7. Critique your commitment to following through. This is something that really matters even after the sale is made and customers say they are happy. Remember, customers are much happier when you follow through.

1. This could be something as simple as promising to have it done in 6 hours and getting it done in 4 hours.

2. It is probably best not to tell any white lies. You will eventually get caught, which will be embarrassing. You will also lose your customers' trust.

NOTES:

4 - Attitude

What is being positive really about?

Some people never have to think about being positive. They are naturally positive, fun-loving, happy-go-lucky individuals who exude enthusiasm and joy. They're the kind of people other people wish they could be. Then there are those who seem to be resigned to a life of misery. They see nothing good around them. The glass is half empty for them. They would rather sit around and complain than take control of their lives. They pity themselves for the hand life has dealt them. Then there are those who want to be positive but have to work at it. They have to make conscious decisions that they are going to be happy. Being positive is an ongoing project for them. Sometimes they succeed and sometimes they don't. This chapter is for this last group of people who want to be positive but need a little help.

Being positive is not just about attitude. It is not as simple as waking up in the morning and telling yourself you are going to have a good day. Some of it is the mental game you play, but a lot of it is about your lifestyle. The way you structure your life determines how you feel about yourself, which in turn contributes to how you feel about life. Your actions directly affect your feelings. You can indirectly influence how you feel by changing your actions. For example, smiling can put you in a good mood. It is hard to fake a smile. When you have a big, genuine smile plastered across your face, you will soon begin to feel the way you look.

Examine the company you keep. Negativity is contagious. If you have dinner with three friends who spend the entire time complaining about being overworked and underpaid, you will most likely join in the conversation even if you started out with a positive attitude. The people around you can drag you down with their negativity or they can lift you up by being positive. You can try to make them more positive by carefully leading the conversation the way you want it to go. However, it might be better to be very selective in choosing your friends. Choose people who see the glass as half full, people who are grateful for their circumstances, people who see possibilities, and who have goals and vision.

If you want to be more positive, commit to it and then tell your friends and family about your decision. Ask them to remind you if you start to sound negative. If you have a problem, you will need all the help you can get. This is retraining your mind behaviorally. People often don't even realize they are being negative. Become aware of how you think and feel by stopping to reflect on how you sound to others.

Next, look at how you treat your body. A healthy body leads to a healthy mind. Do you take care of yourself? Eating a healthy diet and getting regular exercise are crucial to maintaining energy and alertness. When you feel alive and well this is reflected in your attitude. Remember the importance of sleep. Too much or not enough sleep can cause you to be irritable and short-tempered. Cigarettes, alcohol, and other stimulants can also affect your attitude. They can give you a temporary high, but they can also damage your body and attitude.

Stress management is another crucial component to remaining positive. Constant worrying puts you on edge and makes you feel hopeless. Good stress management will help you relax and enjoy life.

The way you treat others will have an impact on how you feel about yourself as well. You get what you give. Helping others will pay off tenfold. You will feel better about yourself because you made time and gave unselfishly. You will also find that when you go out of your way to help others, they will be happy to return the favor to you.

Realize that it is okay to have a bad day. Everyone has a bad day, but never let one bad day lead to another. Plan something for the next day to make sure it is better. Work something into your schedule that you enjoy doing.

You cannot guarantee success in your life, but you can choose how you feel about life. If you feel as if you have been treated unfairly, accept the situation and move on. If you can accept that you didn't get the promotion or didn't make a particular sale, and move on, you are more likely to achieve success. Think about athletes. If a figure skater falls because he or she takes off for a jump where there's a puddle of water; he or she can either keep going, believing a win is still possible, or he or she can sit in the puddle and whine it shouldn't be there. All of the skaters have to deal with the puddle. Some skate around it, some choose not to jump in the puddle, and some take off in the puddle and land their jump in spite of the impediment. They all keep skating with the goal of winning.

Find solutions to the problems in your life so that you can be positive. The solutions could be as extensive as counseling or as simple as making up your mind to forget about the problem because you can't change it. Realize you are in control of your own attitude. Take responsibility for your own life. You can be passive and wait for life to make you happy, or you can be proactive and make your own life happy.

Your attitude toward life is carried over into sales and customer service. It can be measured by your level of passion and respect for what you do. Without passion, it can be hard to get out of bed in the morning. If you are a salesperson who thinks salespeople are pesky and pushy and only out to make money by taking advantage of unsuspecting people, you can't possibly approach your occupation with self-respect. If you respect yourself and what you do, it will show in your attitude and your profits. If you care about what you do, so will the person you are trying to sell to. Passion for your profession will help you persevere through rejection and criticism. Successful people love what they do and honestly believe in their product or service.

Questions

Rate your attitude on a scale of one to ten. One is very negative. Ten is very positive.

How does your lifestyle affect your attitude? Talk about the following categories in terms of what is going wrong or right. If any of these criteria have a negative affect on your attitude, what can you change to make it positive?

1.   Career:

Change:

2.   Home life:

Change:

3.   Exercise:

Change:

4.   Nutrition:

Change:

5.   Health problems:

Change:

6.   Mental health (including stress management):

Change:

7.   Religion/spirituality:

Change:

8.   Friends:

Change:

9.   Rest and Relaxation:

Change:

Answers

1. Think about what is going on in your job right now. Talk about rivalries, competition, problems with your supervisor, lack of productivity, low wages, bad working conditions, etc. How much of this can you control? What can you start doing today to make your life at work more enjoyable?

2. What kinds of problems are you having at home? Maybe life is too hectic, there's too much housework, your kids are having problems in school, you don't spend enough time with your spouse, the bills are stacking up, etc. How can you alter things at home to de-compress and improve your attitude?

3. Exercising is one of the most effective ways to relieve stress. Highly stressed people are generally more negative than people who know how to manage stress. If you don't al-ready do so, what would motivate you to exercise? Describe an environment in which you would be successful at exercising daily.

4. Poor nutrition or food allergies can affect your mood. Describe what you eat, how much you eat, when you eat, and how you feel after you eat. What changes do you need to make to feel better physically? Good physical health contributes to good mental health.

5. Describe any health problems you are experiencing. How do they affect your attitude? Decide what is in your power to change and the steps you will take in order to be posi-tive in spite of the health problems you cannot change.

6. Describe any mental health issues you may be experiencing, including stress. Determine how much of it is under your control? Are you doing everything you can to deal with mental health issues or do you excuse them by blaming them on genetics?

7. Talk just a bit about your religion or spirituality and how it helps you to become more positive. Think of what you could change or keep doing to become even more positive.

8. Sometimes friends can be the source of a negative attitude. It is easy to sit around with friend and complain about work and life. Examine whether or not your closest friends are positive people. Do they help you to be positive or do they influence you to be nega-tive. If they are negative, what can you do to remain positive?

9. Describe what efforts you take to relax and enjoy time away from work. Many worka-holics don't take time to decompress, which means they often become stressed and nega-tive.

5 - Motivation

What is your biggest challenge concerning motivation?

Most people can get motivated whenever they start a new job or implement a new idea. The "newness" is what motivates them. Staying motivated when they run into obstacles, face rejections, burn themselves out, or start questioning their abilities is the biggest challenge. Which of the following statements most closely reflects your course in life?

- I have a vision and control my own life.

- I lack vision and let others control my life.

People are motivated for different reasons. Some seek personal fulfillment. Some want the satisfaction of being a team player working toward a common goal. Others may want money or prestige. Still others are motivated by the chase, or the competition with peers in their own office or the same industry. There are no right or wrong motivations. Perhaps some are nobler than others, but awareness of what motivates you will give you something to fall back on when times are tough.

Setting goals and motivation go hand in hand. Long-term goals are essential. Short-term goals are of equal importance. Set several short-term goals that contribute to achieving your long-term goals. Give yourself time to achieve your long-term goals. Take pride in the little successes you accomplish each day and allow them to build your confidence.

All goals should have a deadline. Give your goals focus by making them specific. A goal of "always try my best" will give you no standard by which to measure its success. A specific goal has a task, a deadline, and an expected outcome. "Make 100 cold calls by Friday" is a specific goal.

Always remind yourself why you set your goals in the first place. Know exactly what you want. Make a list of your goals to serve as a constant reminder. Sometimes people get so caught up in how they're going to accomplish their goals that they forget why they set the goals in the first place. This book will help you maintain the same enthusiasm and motivation you had when you set your goals.

Stress is an enemy of motivation. Stress will plague you with negative energy and distract you from focusing on your goals. Stress makes you tired, and a weary body leads to a weary and ineffective mind. Examine your sources of stress, and then deal with those sources. If you cannot completely resolve those problems, then find a way to alleviate the stress.

Maintaining a positive attitude is the number one key to staying motivated. Surround yourself with people who support your objectives with unbridled enthusiasm. Refuse to keep company with people who say your goals are unrealistic or foolish. These are probably people who are having their destiny controlled by others. Feelings are contagious and associate with negative people will wear you down and detract from your performance. Bear in mind that your choice of friends is part of your overall plan to achieve. Choose friends who speak positively and reaffirm your goals.

Questions

1.   How do you envision your career ten years from now?

2.   What stresses you?

3.   How do you deal with stress?

4.   Are you passionate about your goals? Rate your level of motivation to achieve your goals. 10 is the highest, one is the lowest.

5.   What would help you maintain your motivation long after you have set a goal?

Answers

1. Describe where you think you will be in your career ten years from now. Don't talk about where you *want* to be. Talk about where you think you *will* be if, over the next 10 years, your motivation is the same and you continue the same behaviors you have now. Is that where you want your career to be?

2. Describe the things in all areas of your life that cause you stress. First, talk about the stressful issues you are currently dealing with. Then talk about some things in general that stress you.

3. Sometimes stress just goes away, but more often you have to work at decreasing stress. Describe what you do or can do to relieve your stress. Make an action plan that involves exercise, good nutrition, time to yourself, and better choices regarding family, friends, and co-workers.

4. If you rate your level of motivation for accomplishing your goals as low, you need to examine why. Are your goals unrealistic? Are they concrete? Do you even have goals? Are you unhappy at work? Are you in the wrong line of work? It may be time to re-examine some issues related to work.

5. Determine what motivates you on a day-to-day basis. It's easy to get motivated when you first set a goal, but maintaining that same level of motivation day after day is the challenge. How will you take on that challenge?

6 - Setting Goals

What will happen if you don't set goals?

By setting goals you can turn a seemingly impossible dream into a practical reality. Goals keep you focused on what you really want. Without professional goals you are simply drifting through day-to-day responsibilities, not really headed anywhere specific. It is hard to get motivated when you never have a destination. Without a destination, your journey seems like hard, unexciting work. You are simply going through the motions. Goals give your motions purpose and meaning. Achieving your goals will build lasting confidence, allowing you to set new goals, and further your success.

Be real. The first step is to set realistic goals. Set your goals when you begin a new project or have been inspired by something. This is when adrenaline runs high, and you are excited to begin working toward success. Unfortunately, this adrenaline rush sometimes leads you to set a goal that is unattainable. Set a realistic goal and then set several small goals that will lead to achieving the larger one. Very few people achieve success in one big leap. Success is achieved by taking small steps.

Be specific. Make your goals specific. Vague and undefined goals will lead you astray. If your goal is to "become a leader," how will you define and measure your success? What will keep you on track? What track are you on anyway? If you want to "become a leader," then your goal should be something like "obtain a management position within one year" or "learn enough about baseball to coach my child's little league team next summer." Then, if someone asks you if you achieved your goal, you will be able to answer yes or no. Vague goals leave you open to making excuses, stretching the truth, or interpreting your success any way you want.

Set a deadline. Goals are meaningless if you have until infinity to achieve them. Place a deadline for every goal, whether it's one week, one year, or 30 years. You need to know if you are on track to achieve your goal, and a deadline gives you a criterion for measurement.

Make goals your own. Your goals should be what *you* want to do. Never measure success based on what other people are doing and then try to copy them. That's a plan doomed from the start. You will lose your passion. Set your goals based on what you have accomplished in the past and what you want to accomplish in the future. Your goals should be consistent with your values, beliefs, personality, and what you want out of your personal and professional life.

Write them down. Add weight to your goals by writing them down. Post a copy somewhere so that you can see them each day. Keep a copy in your wallet. Just make sure they are a constant reminder. Check off every goal achieved to show yourself that you are making progress.

Let the world know. Tell other people about your goals – friends, family, co-workers,you're your boss. If possible, find someone who will hold you accountable. Perhaps you and a friend have both set goals. You can check up on each other periodically to note progress and lend support. Having someone you must answer to is a good way to get motivated. This person should be objective and honest. You don't want someone telling you little white lies to make you feel better about yourself when what you really need is a kick in the pants to get on track.

Meet with *numero uno*. That's "number one" for those of you who don't speak Spanish. Schedule a meeting with yourself each week. Take about 30 minutes to work out a plan for what you will accomplish that week. It is important to perform maintenance on your goals each week. If you don't constantly attend to them, you will neglect them and success will never materialize. Set weekly goals that contribute to the big picture. In addition, make notes about last week's goals and think about what went right and what went wrong. Note what might need to be changed and what you can do differently to ensure you succeed in the next week.

Evaluate. What do you do when everything is going wrong? It might be time to think outside the box and self-evaluate. Ask what isn't working and how you can fix it. Know when it is time to change something and when it is simply time to try again. Seek advice from others who know about your goals and from those who have accomplished what you are striving to do. Do everything you can to keep focusing on your goals and how to accomplish them.

Be patient. What do you do when you feel as if you are not getting anywhere? Part of setting realistic goals is setting a realistic time frame in which to accomplish them. People often expect the achievement of goals to be quick and easy. When they find out it's not, they are willing to take the quick and easy road out – they give up. Everyone would like to see success come tomorrow, but that may be too soon. Be willing to wait longer than you had anticipated. Your impatience will only lead to frustration and that will most certainly get in the way of productive work.

Visualize success. Think about what it will be like when you have achieved your goals. How will you feel? Studies of people who achieve their goals show that the most successful people are those who have visualized and expected success all along. What expectations do you have of yourself? Write these down and post them next to your goals.

Work hard. Big goals require hard work. Think of work as your personal challenge. Approach your work with wide-eyed wonder. You can't wait to meet new people every day because there is so much you can learn from them. You can't wait to learn about a new product because it will help make someone's life easier. When planning your week, write down one interesting thing to do each day—something that will either electrify you, appease your curiosity, or help you grow professionally. Be sure to schedule in time for exercise and relaxation. Part of your day should be spent as quiet time, simply doing nothing.

Reward yourself. When you accomplish a goal, reward yourself. Even better, make an agreement with someone else working toward similar goals to reward each other. Rewards should be an occasional treat so that they seem more meaningful. And never cheat by talking yourself into a reward. Never say, "Well, even though I didn't accomplish everything I said I would, I tried really hard this week so I think I deserve to go out to dinner anyway." If you didn't reach your goal, this line of thinking will only trivialize your success when you do reach your goal.

Goals are what separate successful people from people who are merely spectators in life. People who never set goals often live vicariously through the success of others. They can't visualize their own success so they get stuck in a rut, content to just get by. If you are reading this book you are obviously not content to merely get by. You want something more. You are seeking success. Setting goals will help you get what you want.

Questions

1. Do you live vicariously through others? If so, why?

2. Write down three professional goals you have.

a)

b)

c)

3. Write them again only make them more specific.

a)

b)

c)

4. Put a date next to each goal to indicate when you will achieve it.

5. Name three people you will tell about your goals.

a)

b)

c)

6. Name three possible obstacles to achieving these goals.

a)

b)

c)

7. Now describe what you will do to get around these obstacles or deal with them if they come up.

a)

b)

c)

8. Describe what it will be like when you reach your goals.

9. Name three concrete rewards you will give yourself or that someone else will give you when you achieve the three goals described above.

a)

b)

c)

Answers

1. An example of living vicariously is an overzealous father pushing his son to excel at sports. The father didn't make it to the NFL so he'll make sure his son does. If you are living vicariously, you may be more content to admire the success of others than strive to build your own success. You may experience jealously or even anger toward people who have achieved what you feel you can only hope for. If this describes you, what causes you to feel this way? Why do you settle for living vicariously? What goal could you have that would satisfy your need to succeed?

2. Describe your goals in vague terms. What do you want to accomplish in your job? For example, "I want to manage employees someday."

3. Make them more specific. For example, "I want to be the manager of the purchasing department within two years."

4. Try to name people who will hold you accountable and motivate you until you achieve your goals.

5. Think of what may crop up that could make it difficult to achieve those goals. It could be something in your control or something out of your control.

6. No doubt it will feel great to reach a goal. Some people will be satisfied and stop there. However, the most motivated people will immediately set more goals. Which kind of person are you?

7. You may receive a pay raise, more responsibilities at work, perks, bonuses, etc. It may be that you will have to reward yourself. A night out on the town, a vacation, a day at the spa, or maybe just a new book—whatever motivates you to keep going.

7 - Make a Plan Each Day

What does having a plan keep you from doing?

When you get up in the morning, you know just what to do – jump in the shower, get dressed, eat breakfast, brush your teeth, and go to work. It's like playing offense on a soccer team. You know what to do to get to work like a soccer player knows what to do to get the ball in the net. But when you get to work, are you still playing offense? Do you know what to do? Or do you switch to defense waiting for the action to come to you? All those little tasks can seem like one big, overwhelming blur.

Making a plan each day will keep you from operating your business like a soccer goalie standing in front of the net. The ball is yours to kick around. Having a plan gives you motivation, enthusiasm, and direction. It helps to keep you from procrastinating. It shows how you are accomplishing your big goals by taking several small steps. It helps you pay attention to finding work to do instead of thinking about how you might get lucky enough to have work find you. A plan gives you energy because you break down seemingly unachievable goals into attainable tasks. A daily plan makes work less overwhelming.

Prior to each work day, set aside 20 to 30 minutes for yourself. Decide what you will accomplish that day, including appointments, how you will approach those appointments, plans for prospecting, cold calls, networking, and follow ups. Each day you leave the house you need to know where you are going and what you are going to do that day. It doesn't matter if your plan changes midway through the day, just as long as you have a workable plan.

Devise a tentative weekly plan at the beginning of each week. The plan for each day should be based on the weekly plan. Waste no time. Write in something for every hour. Make sure you schedule plenty of time for appointments, and for unexpected free time you should have a list of things to work on. The busier your schedule, the more you succeed. People with busier schedules usually have better time management skills and get more done.

Cross off entries on your plan when you finish them. There is no better satisfaction than looking back at the end of the day and seeing that you didn't just let eight hours go by. You made the most of them by using your time wisely. As the saying goes, "Plan your work and work your plan."

Schedule

Make a sketch of a typical weekly plan. Include meetings with clients, work time, networking time, cold calling, research and/or training time—anything you would expect to do during a week. Also schedule in meals, exercise, family time, etc.

	Monday	Tuesday	Wednesday	Thursday	Friday
7:00 am					
8:00					
9:00					
10:00					
11:00					
12:00 pm					
1:00					
2:00					
3:00					
4:00					
5:00					
6:00					
7:00					
8:00					
9:00					

Tasks: _____

_____

_____

NOTES:

8 - Be a Team Player

Why is it important to be a team player in sales?

Behind every great individual is a good team. Unless you have your own business and work alone, sales is not about how successful *you* can be. It is about how successful your team can be because it's the team that fulfills the company's goals. Many salespeople working for the same company believe that they are in competition with fellow employees. Who can make the most sales? If your employer facilitates this cut-throat atmosphere, it is unfortunate. It may pay off in the short-term, but over the long run, this win-at-any-cost philosophy will reduce productivity to conflict, jealousy, and hostility. Only by helping one another do you ultimately help yourself. You'll enhance your role on the team by helping other team members. You'll become a leader, which earns you even more recognition and respect.

Being a team player means that you must put your own agenda aside for the sake of the company's goals. There should be a healthy balance between achieving your own professional goals and achieving the goals of the company. While individual achievements should be recognized and rewarded, you must remember that those achievements contribute to the bigger picture.

Here are some proven tips for how you can make your team more productive.

Open communication – Keep lines of communication open. Team members should feel free to speak without fear of repercussion. Team members want their voices to be heard. They want to be able to contribute to the end result. Encourage your fellow employees to bring up problems or ideas and listen attentively. Think before you speak. Your comments should always be in the spirit of kindness and cohesiveness. People get defensive when they feel threatened, so stay open-minded.

Frequent communication – All team members should be informed of what is going on at any given time. Information is power and team members feel like part of the group when information is shared freely. Team members must also fully understand what is expected of them. Remember that too many rules and expectations can diminish the team's creativity. All team members should know how their individual efforts contribute to the success of the company.

Focus your competitive spirit – Your desire to compete should be directed at competitors, not fellow teammates. Some people will raise themselves up by bringing down the people around them. You can shine brighter when you help other people shine. The salesperson's credo is that the best way to get what you want is by helping other people get what they want.

Avoid cliquish behavior – Cliques can be unhealthy alliances that split teams apart and lead to animosity. The team ends up performing poorly and treating certain members as outsiders. Low performers become well-liked, while top performers are encouraged to slow down. Watch out for alliances that seem to value friendship over productivity. One solution might be to isolate some team members for a certain amount of time. Then introduce them back into the team after, reminding them about the company's objectives.

Never gossip – Gossip also encourages cliquish behavior. It can cause misunderstandings and resentment among team members. If you have something to say about someone or you are angry with a team member, be a grown up and speak to him or her directly.

Avoid arguments – Arguing is one of the most counterproductive activities a team can engage in. It not only wastes time, it can lead to permanent hostilities. Tone down your voice, avoid sarcasm, and let petty points go. If you feel that a conversation is going to lead to confrontation, leave and come back after you've calmed down and thought about what you'd like to say. Remember that listening and empathy are the best ways to defuse a potentially volatile situation.

Constructive criticism – When you criticize, focus on the person's behavior, not the person. Keep your feedback constructive, friendly, and diplomatic. Always temper feedback with a positive comment about something he or she did right. The person should be left feeling good about him or herself and wanting to improve. Otherwise, the criticism was ineffective and most likely did more harm than good.

Compliment team members – A public compliment will go a long way in establishing rapport and encouraging contributions by other team members. You can compliment a team member in a meeting, in a conversation with their manager, or in an email copied to their manager.

Dealing with different personalities – This can be both a blessing and a curse. Working with different personalities means that you get many different perspectives and experiences for making decisions. It might also mean that some people annoy you, get under your skin, and rub you the wrong way. Never let personality quirks detract from the organization's goals. Just appreciate that it takes all kinds. You don't have to like every kind, but you do have to know how to work with them.

Become decisive – You've heard about the committee that was formed to help the other committee commit, right? Teams can sometimes become ineffective because so much time is spent talking, building team spirit, holding meetings, and making everyone feel special. Teams are formed to be action-oriented. While all of the things mentioned above are important, the team needs to commit to making decisions and taking action. If your team seems to spend endless hours in preparation and not enough time doing, set a timeframe for when a decision will be made and implemented.

Your ability to work within a team has more to do with your attitude toward teamwork than with your skills. You must enjoy working with other people. You must be unselfish, allowing the team to take the glory for your individual accomplishments. We all want to be recognized, but sometimes that recognition will come in the form of the group's success. You must also practice good communication skills and be able to understand how what you say and do affects other people. You may need to keep your personal friendships in check and become aware of how they affect the team atmosphere. Lastly, understand that in the long-term, a team player wins only when everybody wins.

Questions

1. What is your role on your team?

2. Describe your style of communicating with team members. How effective is your style when it comes to building rapport and achieving goals? Explain.

3. Are you competitive? How does this help or harm your team's productivity?

4. How can you avoid becoming part of a clique?

5. What is some good advice for avoiding conflicts with team members?

6. Describe a personality conflict with a co-worker or team member that you've had in the past. How did you deal with it? How would you deal with it today?

7. If your team does not seem very productive, explain what you think the problem is.

8. Do you genuinely enjoy working with other people? Why or why not?

Answers

1. Possible roles might be leader, negotiator, conflict resolver, organizer, problem solver, empathizer, etc.

2. Give an honest critique of your communication style and how effective you are at persuading, negotiating, resolving conflict, getting what you want, and helping other people get what they want.

3. Competition can be both an advantage and a drawback. Competition is good as long as it's not at another team member's expense.

4. Avoid clique behavior like gossiping, ridiculing co-workers, and getting caught up in a web of negativity. Refuse to join in when this behavior takes place around you.

5. Think about conflicts you've had. Think about what you did wrong and what others did wrong when dealing with you.

6. Most likely, you would deal with it differently today. It's anger and feelings of injustice that keep us from dealing with people rationally.

7. Often, a lack of productivity can be traced to personal conflicts between co-workers.

8. Evaluate your level of comfort in dealing with people. Passive-aggressive people are sometimes the hardest personalities to work with. You don't have to like everyone you work with, but you do need to be adult enough to be able to tolerate them and forge a productive working relationship with them.

NOTES:

9 - Time Management

How much is time management really worth?

There aren't enough hours in the day. We hear this all the time, but it's not about the number of hours you work. People seem to think how hard you work is dependent on the number of hours you work. It's more important to work smart, meaning to use the most productive methods to get the job done. If you can work efficiently and in a more organized manner, it will at least *seem* as if there are more hours in the day. Time management skills develop over time. Managing time effectively is a process of trial and error, finding out what works and discarding what doesn't.

The first thing to do is to step back and analyze how you are spending your time. Keep a log that records everything you do – work, get coffee, snack, talk to co-workers, put on make-up, etc. After several days, analyze how much time you spent doing trivial things and how much was devoted to productive work. You might be surprised by how much time you waste.

Next, determine how much your time costs. Write down how much you spend on rent, equipment, administrative costs, and other expenses. In short, how much does it cost per year to run your business? Guess how much profit you will make from your business this year. Then write down how many hours you work in a year. From these figures, calculate an hourly rate. This should tell you how much your time is worth per hour. Looking at it this way, you become more conscious of five-minute coffee breaks, five-minute chats about football at the water cooler, and another five minutes spent reading junk mail.

Decide what your work priorities are. If you find yourself doing a lot of administrative tasks that never produce profit, it may be time to hire an assistant. Make a list of things to do and prioritize the list in order of importance. This will give order to your seemingly endless tasks. If you are in sales, it is best to have a short list of things to do with the goal of completing the list every day.

Here are more tips to help you manage your time:

- Do boring or difficult tasks first. Get these over with so that you can move on to more interesting tasks and allow your enthusiasm to grow as the day goes on.

- Avoid scheduling marathon work sessions. You will only burn out and lose your concentration and passion. Work steadily throughout each day. This is good time management because it prevents procrastination.

- Know what is the best time of day for you. This is when you have the most energy and are the most alert. This is a good time to schedule meetings with customers and prospects. If you find yourself lacking energy most of the day, you may need to change your nutrition or the times and amounts you eat. You might also want to get a physical exam to see if there is a medical reason.

- Work in the same place every day. Familiar surroundings have fewer distractions. Trying to work in a different place every day means you have to adjust to a new environment.

- Minimize noise distractions such as television, music, people talking, etc.

- Avoid working in bed or on the couch. Sit in an ergonomic chair. This will keep you attentive and focused.

- Pay attention to other people who seem to take up your time. People who stop by just to chat and people who call you repeatedly are wasting your time. You can take a minute or two to chat now and then, but some people don't know when to stop and these minutes add up.

- There's a popular saying that goes, "Stress is when your gut says 'no way' and your mouth says 'sure, no problem'." Learn to say no to requests that get you off track. Never let other people waste your time, use your energy, impose on you, or talk you into doing their work for them. It's your time; you have nothing to feel guilty about for not giving it to others every time they ask.

- Making appointments with clients eliminates a lot of wasted time for salespeople. Most clients prefer to work by appointment. It shows the other people you value their time, and it places more value on you as a salesperson.

Staying focused and working hard are good traits to take to work every day. Hard work makes you feel as if you have accomplished something each day. It shapes your attitude for the next workday. It is easier to build on the previous day's success than to make up for the previous day's procrastination. The more you procrastinate, the harder it is to get back into the swing of things. Hard work makes you feel good about your work and your customers will know that. They know who works hard for them and who is just there to make a sale.

Lastly, schedule in some time for relaxation and exercise. This is really the best way to relieve stress. You've heard the doctors say it again and again, but you still can't seem to get yourself to the gym. A lot of time management is really about managing your energy. People with energy seem to have more time. They are less stressed out, and it's stress that makes you feel as if there aren't enough hours in the day. There are enough hours – you just have to arrange your schedule and improve your health in order to use them wisely.

Questions

1. Do you seem to have too much time, not enough time, or just the right amount for work? Explain your answer.

2. Keep a log of everything you do for one day. Then describe how much time was wasted compared to how much was spent productively.

3. Figure out how much your time is worth per hour using the instructions in the book. Then multiply that figure by the number of hours you waste in a day. Does this figure surprise you? Why or why not?

4. What five things can you change to maintain your focus on work?

a)

b)

c)

d)

e)

5. How do you feel about saying "no?" If you have a problem saying "no," how can you overcome it?

6. How do other people waste your time? What can you do to minimize this problem?

1. Consider yourself as a supervisor of you. Now give an honest evaluation of how of effectively you use your time.

Answers

1.   Depending on your answer, you may need to schedule more work or more relaxation. If you seem burned out at the end of the day, it may be time to schedule more relaxation. If you can't pay the bills, it must be time for more work or smarter work habits.

2.   Refer to the chapter. Log everything you do including socializing, phone calls, computer work, going to the bathroom, etc.

3.   Refer to the chapter for instructions.

4.   This could be rearranging your office to avoid looking out the window or hiring an assistant to take care of clerical tasks.

5.   The ability to say "no" can be one of your most important tools at work. People who can't say "no" suffer from a guilt complex. How can you avoid feeling guilty?

6.   Other people can waste your time by chatting with you, asking you to do things that are not your responsibility, playing office politics, etc. Think of limitations you need to put in place and how you can articulate these diplomatically.

7.   Be honest. How much time do you waste talking, eating, making personal calls, writing emails, web surfing, playing computer games, daydreaming, taking care of personal business, etc.

NOTES:

10 - Stress Management

What effect does stress have on your work?

Stress is something most people experience so much but do so little for. Stress management is an absolute necessity for being successful in the long-term. You can get away with running like the wind for a while, but eventually stress will blow you away. It always catches up to people in one way or another, usually in the form of a health problem. Stress can sap your energy, make you unfocused, and lead to health problems, including headaches, insomnia, ulcers, high blood pressure, and heart disease.

How does this translate to your job? Stress affects the quality of your work. If you are frazzled by your job you will seem as if you're in a hurry to get it over with. However, some stress is good. Without some stress people become bored and lazy. Positive stress adds anticipation and excitement to your job. It can motivate you to achieve. If you love what you do and know how to manage your stress, it will show in the form of confidence and eagerness to perform your tasks. Negative stress will eventually cause you to burn out, affecting your profits and making you professionally ineffective.

Negative stress not only affects your body, it affects your attitude. The way you feel about yourself, both mentally and physically, will be reflected in your ability to provide quality service. This chapter will give you some tips on how to alleviate negative stress.

Don't be a workaholic. Stress management involves balancing work, family, and fun. Some people think it's okay, even noble, to work evenings and weekends. They brag about how many hours they work in a week as if they have something to show off. They may even justify an excessive amount of work by claiming that it's not really work because it is fun and they enjoy it. That may be, but it is still work. It's still time you are not taking to relax, to be with your family, and to participate in exercise and hobbies. Stick to a balanced work schedule and devote an ample amount of time to rest, leisure activities, and your family.

Exercise. That dreaded word, yet there is no better stress reliever than cardiovascular exercise. Getting motivated to exercise is the challenge. Getting out of bed an hour early is the hardest part. Once you've done it you are happy you did. Exercise needs to be fun. Try exercising in aerobic or kickboxing classes. Exercising with friends makes the experience more entertaining. Or join an adult basketball or softball team. Or connect with co-workers to exercise at lunchtime. Do anything to make it fun.

Practice relaxation techniques. Yoga, visual imagery, quiet time, deep breathing exercises, muscle relaxation exercises, meditation, massage therapy, and biofeedback are all activities that can help you relax.

Maintain good nutrition. Most of us know what's good for us and what's bad for us. If you don't, it's time to consult your doctor or a nutritionist. Evaluate whether what you put in your mouth is helping you maintaining adequate energy levels to perform your work effectively.

Avoid stimulants. Caffeine, nicotine, alcohol, and refined sugar speed up the heart and cause a variety of other changes in your body. Most of the time the long-term health risks do not justify the short-term stimulation. Avoid them as much as possible.

Laugh. Smiling and laughing inevitably affect your attitude and stress level. They make tasks seem more enjoyable. Probably what you do in a day is not actually a life or death situation so don't treat it like one. And remember the old saying, "The world is a mirror when you wear a smile."

Get organized. If you get stressed about all the small tasks that have to get done, perhaps it is time to hire an assistant. Or, take a few minutes at the beginning of each day to get organized. Knowledge is power and when you know what you have to do, you are empowered.

Become aware of your stressors. Some people find keeping a journal helps them pinpoint their stressors. Once you know what your stressors are, become conscious of them on a daily basis and observe how you react to them.

Consult with professionals. Doctors, psychologists, fitness trainers, career counselors, clinical social workers… these are all people who can help you manage your stress.

Find a mentor. Having someone who can provide you with insight about your professional or personal life allows you to see your life from a different perspective. You may find that someone who can offer you objective advice will become an invaluable part of your success.

Choose your friends carefully. If your friends are the cause of your stress, they probably aren't worth keeping as friends. If family members are the source of stress, structure your life in such a way that you can deal with them. For example, if your mother-in-law calls you every night complaining about every bad thing that ever happened to her, get caller ID or suggest to her that she find another way to deal with her problems. You never have to add to your stress by taking on someone else's stress. Everybody is responsible for their own feelings.

Stress doesn't have to interfere with your professional goals. The more you work at reducing stress the better you will feel. You must be proactive. Don't wait for something magical to come along and sweep you off your feet. Get busy making a plan to exercise, eat right, engage in a relaxing activity, get organized, and manage your relationships. When it comes to stress management, you need to put a little work into it. You will decrease your stress if you make the necessary changes in your life.

Questions

1. Describe your level of stress.

2. How does stress affect your work performance?

3. Do you think it's noble to work extra hours? How can you enforce a balanced work schedule for yourself?

4. Describe your exercise schedule. If you don't exercise regularly, write your excuse here.

5. Describe your diet. Explain how the foods and stimulants you ingest affect your energy level.

6. Are you aware of what things stress you? List them here.

7. Do you have a plan for managing your stress? Describe your plan.

Answers

1. Think about your energy level, your physical health, your mental health, the time you spend with friends and family, your money problems, how much you exercise, etc. Rate your stress level on a scale of one to ten. Ten is the highest.

2. This is a question that asks you to evaluate how much more productive could you be without negative stress.

3. If you are missing time with your family, experiencing stress-related ailments, or do not seem to be having fun anymore, then you may want to take a look at balancing your schedule.

4. Imagine you are in the hospital after having a heart attack because you didn't exercise. How would your excuse hold up?

5. This may take some research. Do foods with sugar cause you to lose focus at work?

6. Refer to answer number one. What are your stressors?

7. A plan would include financial security, family issues, job satisfaction, leisure time, exercise, nutrition, friends, and physical and mental health.

The Sales Giant

NOTES:

_____

_____

_____

_____

_____

_____

_____

_____

_____

_____

_____

_____

_____

_____

_____

_____

_____

_____

_____

_____

_____

11 - Courage

What is the one thing you need to do to conquer your fears?

You have a brain. You have a heart. Now all you need is some courage. Fear of failure is perhaps the strongest force working against motivation and a positive attitude. Fear of failure can make it almost impossible to fulfill your goals. Instead, it can cripple progress and prevent success. Failure is nothing new. Throughout history, humans have learned through trial and error. Everyone in history has made mistakes, but only the successful people learned from them. Why should your method of learning be any different? Even the greatest scientists rarely got it right the first time. It took Thomas Edison 10,000 tries to get the first light bulb to work. Innovators like Edison are great because they kept trying.

For many people it is the fear of criticism that immobilizes them. This demonstrates a lack of confidence. Try not to think of criticism as a personal attack on your character or capabilities. Instead, think of it as feedback. Successful people use feedback to learn and to try new approaches.

Never waste precious time trying to conquer fear before you take action. Do just the opposite. Take action in order to fight your fears. Do the very thing you are afraid of. Hundreds of surveys show that the number one fear is speaking in public. There is no better remedy for this fear than taking a public speaking class. The more you do something, the less you will be afraid of it. Procrastination is sometimes about being lazy, but just as often it is about fear. Procrastinators mistakenly hope that by tomorrow something will change to make a task easier and less intimidating. Maybe someone will come along to give you a break, and you won't have to work so hard or risk so much. Successful people know that acting quickly on an unpleasant task is the best answer. Act now.

Keep realistic expectations. This will help you to try and try again. Never give up after the first try if you don't get the result you expect. Believe that every result of every try is in some way moving forward. Even if the benefits are not tangible, you are always learning something valuable for the future. At least you are learning what doesn't work. Persistence pays off.

On the other hand, be willing to try something new when it becomes clear your way is not effective. Some people give up. If your way isn't working, take what you have learned and apply it to new ways of thinking and doing. Ask how the mistake happened, how it could have been prevented, and what you can do better next time.

Never take failure personally. *You* are not a failure unless you accept failure. If one of your ideas failed, that's okay. And maybe that idea wasn't a complete failure. It may have been the stepping stone to a better idea. Failures don't mean anything if you succeed eventually. Most successful people have several failures under their belt.

If you are a "what if" person, who is always expecting the worst to happen, then go ahead and visualize the worst possible outcome you can think of. But don't stop there. Decide how you will deal with it if it does happen. Most likely, you will realize that even the worst case scenarios aren't as bad as you think. Anxiety is often caused by the perception that you will not be able to handle unexpected situations. When you break down that anxiety to examine its components, you often find your fears are irrational and that you are perfectly capable of dealing with failure.

Change can be very unsettling. Risk is involved and the results of taking risks can be good or bad. However, only by taking risks can you achieve success. Even if you never get the outcome you wanted, you still have gained because you come away with a better understanding of your strengths and weaknesses.

The last words of advice on fear—keep a sense of humor. If you don't already have one, get one. People who can laugh at their mistakes are more likely to move on with a positive attitude.

You have the power to overcome fear by changing the way you think about it. If your life seems to be run by fear, you need to develop some new thought processes and behavioral strategies to deal with it. Never be a spectator and allow fear to control you. You need an action plan—namely, namely, to do the very thing you are afraid of. If you wish to succeed, the only thing you should be afraid of is fear taking over your life.

Questions

1. How do failures and setbacks affect you? What is your thought process when something does go the way you expect it to?

2. Think of a significant failure in your career (a demotion, a lost sale, getting fired). How did it affect your motivation?

3. Do you handle criticism well? Why or why not?

4. When you are afraid to do something, how do you deal with that fear?

5. Think of something you succeeded at because you refused to give up?

6. Think of something you usually procrastinate doing because of fear. Then make a list of "what if" questions. Then decide how you will handle each "what if".

What if…

How you will handle it –

What if…

How you will handle it --

What if…

How you will handle it –

7.   How do you feel about changes in your work place?

8.   How do you feel about taking risks?

Answers

1. Describe how you react (both mentally and behaviorally) when you are disappointed something didn't happen the way you wanted it to.

2. Talk about how you deal with significant failures? Do they affect you for the short-term or does it take a long time to get over them?

3. Many people take criticism personally. Describe how you feel when you are criticized. Are you able to maintain your motivation? Does criticism motivate you even more? If so, is it good or bad motivation? Does it make you *want* to do better or make you fear not doing better?

4. Describe your thought process and your actions when you are afraid of something related to work.

5. This is your time to boast. Tell about something you are particularly proud of because you persevered when you could have given up.

6. Cold calling is an example of something that many people procrastinate. Possible "what if" scenarios include the following:

    a. **What if** they get mad at me for taking up their time?

    How you can handle it – Politely thank them for their time and move on to the next call before you have time to dwell on their rudeness.

    b. **What if** they threaten to spread bad news about my company if I ever call again?

    How you can handle it – Politely thank them for their time and cross them off your list so you never call again. Move on to the next customer.

    c. **What if** I get tongue-tied and can't think of anything to say once they're on the phone?

    How you can handle it – If you are a beginner, prepare your conversation ahead of time. For a while, you may want to work with a script. You can also rehearse it with another person.

7. Describe your level of comfort with change. How do you react to changes at work? Do you initiate and support change or do you resist it?

8. Describe your level of comfort with risk-taking. If someone said they were going to take a risk that could double your salary if it worked but cut your salary in half if it didn't work, how would you respond?

12 - First Impression

How long does it take to form an opinion of someone?

It is often said that the first four minutes of contact with someone is all you need to formulate your opinion of him or her. In a book entitled, *Contact: The First Four Minutes*, several people were studied in social situations and how they interacted with one another during the first four minutes. People walked away from those who did not make a good impression within four minutes. Those who made a good impression and were able to connect to the other person were engaged in further conversation.

Sales is one setting where the first four minutes count. What you say, how you present yourself, how you shake hands, how you dress, even how you comb your hair, all contribute to the other person's assessment of you, your abilities, and your trustworthiness.

Approach an introduction in an enthusiastic mood. Make up your mind that you're going to be happy that day, and you can't wait to meet this prospect for the first time. Maintain eye contact with him or her. This shows that you want to get to know him or her better. Looking out the window or staring at the carpet conveys a lack of confidence. When you project confidence from the inside out, you will find that others have confidence in you.

Never be overconfident. This is not your opportunity to let everyone know how good you are. You want to let them know how important *they* are. If they are the talkative type, let them talk to their hearts' content. If they seem reserved, ask questions to bring them into the conversation. Listen attentively and respond to what they say intelligently. First impressions should be a two-way street. A good first impression is a natural and engaging interaction between two people, so get the other person involved. The more natural you appear, the more your prospects will feel at ease.

If you meet someone at his or her office, comment on something you see—preferably something you have an interest in. This will break the ice and help you establish rapport. Use humor whenever possible, but be tasteful. As a general rule, sarcasm and cynicism are not a good idea. Laugh at their jokes, even if you don't find them funny. There is nothing more awkward and embarrassing than telling a joke and not getting a laugh.

Then begin asking questions related to business. Ask basic questions like how many employees they have, what they consider the most successful aspect of their business, how a certain product is made, or the process for doing a particular job. They are merely questions that help you start thinking about how you can help their business. In retail, you will probably skip the questions about hobbies and interests and go right into asking them what they are looking for; what size, color, shape, style; in what price range; and if there is anything else they need.

First impressions are equally important in a store setting. If you are huddled in a corner with co-workers gossiping instead of attending to customers, you have sent them the message that their patronage is not important. Likewise, the failure to acknowledge a customer standing in front of you with a simple, "I'll be with you in a moment," while you finish writing a note to yourself is bad service. They're thinking, "Hello. Can you see me? Am I invisible?" People are in a hurry but most are willing to wait if their presence is acknowledged.

A good employee is enthusiastic, eager, conscientious, and genuinely cares about people. A bad employee is bored, disinterested, and only there for a paycheck. Most people can learn to make good first impressions, but sometimes you have to work at it in the beginning.

Believe in the power of making a good first impression. Pay attention to the details of your physical appearance and your body language. Think before you speak. One little mistake can be the only thing customers remember about the first meeting. Bad first impressions make a lasting impact. People who make a good first impression get invited back. They will then have another chance to reinforce that good impression.

Questions

1.   Take a look at yourself in a mirror just before going to work. What are three things you admire and three things you would change?

Admire

a)

b)

c)

Change

a)

b)

c)

2.   Focusing just on appearance, body language, and the things you say, would you buy from someone like you? Why or why not?

3.   What are three specific things you will focus on to make a good first impression?

a)

b)

c)

4.   Discuss your level of confidence. What do you do that may convey a lack of confidence?

5.   What are three questions you can ask a shy person to help keep the introductory conversation going?

a)

b)

c)

6.   Describe your sense of humor. Is it appropriate for a good first impression?

Answers

1.   Consider what you realistically have the power to change.

2.   This is an honest critique of yourself. Pretend you don't know you, and you are getting a first impression of yourself.

3.   These will relate to external factors like clothes, make-up, and grooming.

4.   Think about nervous habits, speech problems, and body language.

5.   Don't get too personal. Shy people will get embarrassed or even offended. Ask basic questions, such as "What sports do you like?"

6.   Evaluate your sense of humor objectively. Is it cynical or sarcastic? Does it consist of a dry wit, jokes, a funny story, or a good belly laugh over a bottle of rum?

13 - Appearance

What do proper dress and grooming habits result in?

Image is everything when it comes to sales. You never get a second chance to make a first impression, so you want to make a good one. Many employers are moving away from business casual dress codes and requiring suits and ties instead. This is especially important in sales. Study after study illustrates that proper dress and grooming habits result in a positive image for a company—more time in meetings, and increased sales.

Attention to the way you dress goes a long way toward establishing trust and rapport with potential customers. People are looking for credibility in their choice of a company. They want someone who presents a professional and reliable image. Your business attire can either reinforce or contradict that image.

It is not just what you wear that counts. Uncombed hair, gaudy mascara, a five o'clock shadow, dirty fingernails, a purple tongue from sucking on lollipops, you name it—it all contribute to the overall impression you make.

Some salespeople recommend that you look as much as possible like the person to whom you are making a sale. However, most recommend that you dress at least one step up. It is always better to be overdressed than underdressed. The right clothes can make you feel more secure in how you approach a sale. If you know you are dressed well, your attitude improves and your self-confidence increases. You reflect your line of work positively by portraying a professional image.

There are no rules set in stone about how salespeople should dress. Each organization needs to assess its own standards. Some general guidelines for how to dress are:

- Choose accessories that compliment your clothes and do not distract your audience's attention. Big, dangling, shiny earrings can transfix a customer's attention on your ears instead of on what you are saying.

- Match your shoes to your wardrobe. It might be raining outside but rubber galoshes with your skirt and blouse won't work.

- Take care of your footwear. Shine your shoes. Scuff marks on shoes show you never have the time or care enough about yourself to take care of your wardrobe.

- No open-toed shoes, not even in the summer. Save your sandals for the next Woodstock reunion.

- No short skirts. All skirts should be at least below the knees.

- No bare midriffs. If you're a saleswoman, most likely your teenage years are over. The only exception would be if you are a teen selling similar fashions to other teens.

- Your clothes should compliment your body shape. Consult with a fashion expert to find out what is most flattering for your shape and size.

- Dress conservatively. Big flowers or sailboats on your shirt might be cute and reflect your personal hobbies, but they are out of line with appropriate attire for most sales.

- Men should wear a white t-shirt under their button up shirt. You might be proud of what's under that shirt, but your clients don't need to see it through your dress shirt.

- Be up-to-date. If your suit looks like what your grandfather wore for his wedding, it's time to buy a new one. Consult with professionals who can recommend a modern, well-fitting wardrobe.

- Iron your clothes. Wrinkled clothing is tacky and unprofessional.

- Remove lint from clothing. If you are covered in dog hair, go fetch a lint roller.

What to do about those unexpected in-person calls from potential customers? Keep a back-up formal outfit and casual outfit in your closet at work for unanticipated visits. If it's a particularly hot month, you might consider keeping an extra shirt or two at your office to change into during the day.

The bottom line is that you want people to be impressed by your image and focused on your message, not on your clothes. Spend a little extra time thinking through what you can do to improve your image. Look at yourself in a mirror and ask whether you would buy from someone like yourself. Use fashion experts to help you find what is right for you. Never underestimate the importance of details. If you look the part, you will play the part much more convincingly.

Questions

1. Compare and contrast the way you dress with the way your customers dress. Are you dressed more formally? Do your clothes convey credibility?

2. Do your clothes help you feel confident? Why or why not?

3. List three details you could improve upon and how you will improve them. Examples: clean fingernails, less eye shadow, trimmed nose hairs, etc.

a)

b)

c)

4. Do you know what kind of clothes compliment your body shape? If so, what type? If not, how can you find out?

Answers

1.   You need to dress one step up from your customers. Otherwise, you will not be perceived as professional or credible.

2.   Discuss how your clothes make you feel relative to the type of business you are in. Do you feel professional? Do you take pride in the way you dress?

3.   All the details count. Where do you fall short?

4.   Describe your body shape and your clothes. Ask someone else's opinion of whether or not your clothes compliment your shape.

14 - Keep it Neat

What might customers fear if they see a messy office?

First impressions can make or break a sale. If you've got mud on your carpet, papers scattered about, holes in your couch cushions, dead plants, and radical political posters on the walls, you may want to re-evaluate the image your office sends to potential customers. If you meet with prospects and customers at your place of business it is crucial that you present a neat, clean, and professional image. What customers see in your environment will shape their concept of you and how you conduct business. A messy office could make them fearful of a careless business transaction. On the other hand, a clean office will make them believe that you take pride in your professional appearance.

Start with the basics. Do you have papers scattered around? Are bags, briefcases and coats thrown in the corner? Are there crusts of bread and orange peels on your desk? These are all things you can take care of by using the file cabinet, closet, and garbage can.

Next, look for the bigger things that make the office seem untidy. Do computer wires protrude into public view? Do you have piles of folders on the floor? Is the office cluttered with junk you bought at garage sales? Do the pigeons poop on your window ledge? These are all noticeable features that say, "I don't have time to be bothered with the mess." And your customers may not have time to be bothered with you.

Then look for things that don't necessarily seem messy but make your office look as if it's been unloaded from the truck of a second-hand store. Is the carpet worn and frayed? Are there holes in the walls? Is the cover missing from the light fixture? Does the doorknob turn? You may need to invest some money, but it will pay for itself in increased sales.

If your office is a place where you make sales, think about distractions in the office. You want the person to pay attention to you, not read a poster on World Series statistics or on 101 things to flush down the toilet. You need a few things in your office that reflect your personality and interests. Those can serve as a way to begin a conversation if the customer notices them and chooses to comment on them. However, choose items that will not detract attention excessively, such as posters with things that seem peculiar, things that take a long time to read, or those posters that are supposed to form a picture if you stare at them long enough.

On the other hand, you can help put people at ease by making your office homey. A fireplace would be nice, but most of us can't afford that luxury. So instead, you can bring in comfortable chairs, pictures of nature that seem relaxing, plants, soft lighting, and other items that have a quiet, gentle feel to them.

Also be careful about placing brochures and other advertising items where customers can see them. They may feel free to take one and start reading it while you are speaking. The end of a meeting is when you hand them materials to take with them and look over. These materials should summarize what you have told them in a meeting.

Remember, everything you do, everything you say, and everything customers see contribute to shaping their image of you and your company. Do not overlook and underestimate the power of small things like a clean and uncluttered office. You basically have four minutes to win them over. Even if you have a delightful personality, your prospect's positive image of you can be erased even as they are tripping over that power cord. Start cleaning today!

Questions

1. Look around your office. What are three things that could be considered controversial or inappropriate for a salesperson?

a)

b)

c)

2. Still looking around your office, what are three things that are worn out and need to be fixed or replaced?

3. What are three things in your office that reflect your hobbies and interests that could help start a conversation?

4. Imagine you are a customer who has never seen your office. Walk in and jot down your first impressions of your office.

5. What image does your office convey?

6. Is that image consistent with your goals? Why or why not?

7. Would you want to buy from someone who had an office like yours? Why or why not?

Answers

1. Look for political or religious objects primarily, anything that could ignite a heated discussion or offend somebody.

2. Can you afford to replace them? Or is it that you just haven't gotten around to replacing them yet?

3. Don't think too hard when doing this. What do your eyes go to first? Is that where you want them to go?

4. Jot down some adjectives that describe your office. To help you get started—is it clean, professional, boring, New Age, childish…?

5. Think about what you want the image of your business to be and whether your office reflects that.

6. Consider what your standards are when you make purchases and whether you meet your own standards. Or do you expect less of yourself?

NOTES:

Successful Prospecting

15 - Prospecting

What can a lack of prospects lead you to do?

Prospecting is like putting money into a savings account. It's insurance and it's assurance that you will always have customers. Continuously searching for customers keeps each individual sale from seeming like a life or death situation. Lack of prospects can sometimes push a salesperson into desperate situations, like drastically discounting a product or service just to make a sale. Prospecting means there are always potential customers on the horizon so there's no need to panic. Some days feel like a feast or a famine. A good prospecting plan and the discipline to follow through will overcome that feeling.

Find the audience you wish to target and focus on it. Always prospect. Decide on the number of people with whom you make contact each day. Set prospecting goals, and keep an organized record of who you will call and when you will call them. Document your results each day and evaluate whether you need to increase your activity based on your level of success.

Never waste your time on people who are not interested. Some people will put you off or lead you on. Be willing to let go of people who seem insincere or who maintain a casual interest for too long without committing.

When someone gives you a lead, follow up on it immediately. The best time to prospect is right after you make a sale. This is when your enthusiasm, motivation, and energy are high. Your attitude toward the lead is positive because you see it as an opportunity. When a lead gets put at the bottom of the list, it is reduced to one more thing you need to get out of the way. Pursue the lead as soon as you get it. Never treat it like a chore.

Remember, sales is a numbers game. Each business generates its own set of numbers. Keeping accurate records will help you discover how many prospecting calls it will take to make a presentation and how many presentations it will take to make a sale. Prospecting is your business insurance. Never become so comfortable with your current crop of customers that you put off adding to your base. Consider prospecting an everyday part of business and your business will profit over the long-term.

Questions

1.	Do you feel as if each sale is a life or death situation? Why or why not?

2.	How many people will you contact each day?

3.	What three steps will you take to deal with people who don't seem very interested in what you offer?

a)

b)

c)

4.	How will you make sure that you will follow up on a lead right away?

Answers

1. If you feel like you are making compromises you don't really want to make, you probably need to do more prospecting.

2. This number will depend on the nature of your business and on your advertising strategies.

3. You need to ask more questions until they tell you what they need. Also, you may consider presenting the product to show how it will benefit the customer.

4. Devise a strategy for following leads. This might entail following all leads within 24 hours. Making contact with all leads immediately and then following up later. Or hiring an assistant to follow up on leads.

16 - Generate a List of Prospects

Where do new customers come from?

The best way to ensure a continued high level of sales is to have a large number of prospects to draw from. Great salespeople are always adding new prospects to replace lost customers.

Got prospects? If not, these suggestions will do your sales good.

- Set up a table at the entrance where customers enter. Ask them to drop a business card into a fishbowl. Then, hold a drawing for store merchandise.

- Collect business cards at meetings, luncheons, dinners, parties, etc.

- Buy mailings lists off the Internet or from the phone company

- Buy exhibit space at a trade show. Hold a contest offering a prize.

- Conduct a seminar or workshop on a subject in which you are an expert. Collect names and addresses from the registration list.

- Be a guest speaker at an organizational meeting. Collect business cards.

- Request a name and address from anyone who calls your business.

- Request a name and address on comment slips for your suggestion box.

- Offer a free newsletter or catalog and use the subscription list for marketing.

- Work with other businesses to exchange customer lists.

- All purchases should include a customer feedback form. Request a name and address on the form.

- Keep the name and address of anyone who writes your business asking for information.

- Offer existing customers a discount or gift certificate for referrals.

- Exchange business cards at Chambers of Commerce Greeters or other business gatherings.

The best way to get new customers is to use your existing customers. They can give you tips and referrals but usually only if you ask for them or offer an incentive. It can be easier to establish rapport with word-of-mouth referrals because these customers already have a trusting relationship with the person who referred them. Often this translates into trust in the salesperson.

You must continuously build your customer base. Customers come and go. A continuous effort to add to your customer list will prevent a shortage when more customers go than come. Always be on the lookout for potential customers and your supply will never be exhausted.

Questions

1.   Think of three ways you can collect business cards where you work.

a)

b)

c)

2.   What other ways can you attract new customers to your business?

3.   What subject(s) are you an expert in that you could share with others in a seminar, work-shop, or as a guest speaker?

4.   What are three incentives you could offer customers to give you leads and referrals?

a)

b)

c)

Answers

1. Possible answers might include: asking for them, holding a drawing, offering your card first in exchange, etc.

2. Offer incentives for referrals, advertise a special, give out gift certificates, offer a free seminar, etc.

3. Name a few things you could talk about. If you own an art supply store, you could offer a seminar on painting pottery, drawing still lifes, a children's class, or a seminar on your experience as a small business owner.

4. Possible benefits might be: gift certificates, discounts, coupons, an award, etc.

17 - Building on Your Customer Base

How can you get your current customers to help you find new customers?

You could do all the work yourself but why would you want to? Why not get new customers by enlisting the help of your current customers? Give your customers incentives for referring you to their friends and family, and you could be in big business.

The number one car salesman in the world is Joe Girard. Yes, he's really number one in terms of how many cars he sells in a year. He gives customers $25 for every person who sends someone to him to buy a car. He calls them "bird dogs." His bird dog expenses amount to about $14,000 a year, but he pays only half of that out of his own pocket since it is tax deductible. The $7,000 he spends more than pays for itself. The point is that you can generate a lot of business by offering incentives. Some customers will recommend you because they are pleased with your service. That should always be a priority—pleasing customers. Other customers don't have time to sell for you, but will make the time if you give them a reason to. In some industries and some states this may not be legal. Check with your state regulatory agency.

It doesn't have to be cash. You can offer a credit at your store, a gift certificate, free publicity, a testimonial for their own business, or a gift. The goal is to reward customers for rewarding you. They reward you every time they recommend you. Unfortunately, rewarding people is something we don't often think to do, but it is the best way to reinforce good behavior.

You can get customers to sell for you in indirect ways too. Ask them for a written, taped, or filmed testimonial. These lend credibility on the selling stage. Everyone can toot his or her own horn about a product, but hearing praise from a prominent company or person who uses your product adds much more weight to what you say.

Gather stories about how your product or service benefited an individual or a company. Ask people to talk about more than just numbers and statistics. Ask them to include how the product or the changes the product caused made them feel. These types of stories make the experience seem real. People buy based on emotions, not logic. They use logic to justify their emotions. Real life stories connect with that emotional place.

Another suggestion is to gather business cards from customers and have them write one or two reasons why they chose to buy from you on the back of the card. This is an easy way to show a prospect several clients at once and what they said about you. Put them in plastic sheets in a 3-ring binder. Your customers like to have their business card displayed. Put all your testimonials, reference letters, and stories in the binder to make a testimonial portfolio.

One of the keys to great salesmanship is establishing a reciprocal relationship. When you can, offer to give a testimonial to a customer's business in return for his or her time and effort. Always thank people for their testimonial in writing.

The last point is to let people know that you want referrals. The people who get the most referrals are often the ones who ask for them. A veterinarian made it easy for people. He had a stack of informational cards at the front desk that said, "If you are happy with our service, please take a few cards and pass them out to your friends." This veterinarian knows that he won't get referrals if he doesn't ask for them. People won't necessarily think to do it themselves, so make it easy for them.

Finally, after the sale is final and all arrangements for the delivery of the product are made, say something like, "Well Bill, before I go let me ask you for a little help. As a salesperson you know the most important assets I have are prospective clients. Who else do you know that would want to experience the joy of buying from me? Do you know anyone that I could call on that may be interested in this product?" At this point, do not say anything. Wait for the customer to answer the question. It may surprise you to see the customer pull out a book or a list of people he or she knows and go through it name by name. All you should do is keep writing until he or she is done.

Questions

1.   What are three incentives you can offer customers for recommending you?

a)

b)

c)

2.   What is your method for collecting testimonials?

3.   Write down one testimonial you have on file. Would this testimonial make you want to buy from you if you didn't know anything about your business?

4.   Name three possible people or businesses you could exchange testimonials with.

a)

b)

c)

5.   What is one way you can ask customers for referrals?

Answers

1.   One possibility would be a discount on his or her next purchase. Think of some more incentives that your business can realistically offer.

2.   Determine which kind of testimonial would be most effective for your type of business. The kinds might include: written, tape recorded, or videotaped.

3.   After writing down the testimonial, look at it as if you don't know anything about your business or about the customer who gave you the testimonial. Decide if it is persuasive enough to persuade you to buy from your business.

4.   Think about people you have done business with, people who owe you a favor, or friends who own a business.

5.   Ask your customers to help you by referring their friends and family to your business.

NOTES:

_____

_____

_____

_____

_____

_____

_____

_____

_____

_____

_____

_____

_____

_____

_____

_____

_____

_____

_____

_____

_____

_____

_____

18 - How to Get Referrals

How much of your business can be generated by referrals?

Referrals can be your lifeline to continued success. Some studies show that as much as 90 percent of all business comes from referrals. Most people talk with friends about what they got, where they got it, and how much they paid for it. You hear these conversations all the time. People give referrals without thinking twice. However, this doesn't mean you should assume that referrals will simply come to you. Sometimes you have to ask for them.

Acquiring referrals is where forming a strong relationship and establishing trust with your customers becomes important. The stronger the loyalty, the more passionate a customer will be about urging a friend or family member to do business with you.

It is also important to educate your customers about your products or services. When you are selling to them, point out the features and benefits as much as possible. The more they know, the better they can convince their friends to do business with you. They will basically do the selling for you before the customer even arrives at your store.

Ask for referrals at the right time. When customers are particularly pleased with your service, or have expressed the usefulness of an item, or just feel comfortable talking with you, tell them that you would appreciate them mentioning you if they know of someone in the market for what you sell. You have earned their trust, and they will believe you give all your customers the same courtesy and dedication that you gave them.

Indeed, treat all your customers equally no matter how large or small the account. You never know when a small account has wealthy connections that can give you larger accounts. It's not the size of the account that matters; it's the *potential* size of the account. What customers emphasize the most when making a referral is not the product itself, but fair, friendly, and responsive service.

If you are going to meet a prospect that was referred to you, always introduce yourself by mentioning the name of the person who referred you. "Ms. Rainer suggested I call on you..." However, don't think that this alone will get you through the door. You should also try to learn as much as possible about the prospect. Just because you know someone who knows someone doesn't mean that someone will be impressed by you. Do your research before going into a presentation.

Be sure to thank customers when they give you a referral. Thank them even if it doesn't work out because you want to keep the referrals coming in the future. Cash, bonuses, discounts, gift certificates, and merchandise are all good ways to motivate people to mention you.

Questions

1.   Do you know how much of your business comes from referrals? If so, how much?

2.   Describe your method for finding out where referrals come from.

3.   Do you treat all your customers the same way? Give an honest description of how you may treat customers differently.

4.   Do you think a referral is a free ride to a sale? How should you prepare for meeting with someone who was referred to you?

Answers

1. When you get new customers you should ask them how they heard about you. Record how many are from referrals and how many are from other sources.

2. A couple of ways to find out are to ask them verbally or to give them a customer satisfaction card.

3. We may say that all customers should be treated equally. But if you are a real estate agent and you have a client looking for a house for $80,000 and another client looking for a house for $8,000,000, do you give them the same amount of time, effort, and courtesy?

4. The answer to this question is that you should prepare the same way you would for any other customer.

19 - Networking

What is networking really about?

Zig Ziglar tells us, "You can get what you want out of life if you just help enough people get what they want." That is the approach a businessperson must take when networking. Networking is not about making sales; it's about making connections. Those connections may indeed become customers, but they may be more effective in providing referrals or simply providing moral support to you and your business. You never know how a connection will help you.

Networking is a two-way street. You can ask other businesspeople for help with your business but only if you have something to offer them. If there is no mutual benefit, you are not really networking. It is best if you can help them first and then ask for a return favor in the future.

Networking is not a time for high-pressure sales tactics. Actually, there is never a time for high-pressure sales tactics, but especially not when you are networking. You want to show that you understand and care about other people and their business. (Use the tips offered in the chapter about establishing rapport.) You want to form long-term business relationships that will help you and your business grow throughout the years.

There are many benefits to a professional network. A network can help you keep informed about possible prospects, about events in the area, about new technology, about your competitors, or about ways to increase productivity. A network can offer advice, boost your self-confidence, and form friendships.

Before you attend a networking session, decide whom you would like to meet. Decide on some topics you will try to discuss with the people you plan to meet. Be interesting. Don't recite the plot of a movie you saw the night before. Talk about subjects that will interest a businessperson, like marketing strategies or local community events. Ask for a reservation list before the event occurs and try to learn something about the guests and their businesses before you arrive. Plan your opening questions and think of tips, information, or leads that can benefit them. You are not there to sell; you are there to make contacts and exchange ideas.

When you are in a networking event, smile and look as if you are eager to be there. Be approachable. You want people to remember you, so wear a nametag that clearly states your name, business, and what you do. Shake hands firmly but don't make it a death grip. Introduce yourself clearly and state what you do. This should take no more than 10 seconds.

Keep moving around the room. Never spend too much time with one person. The point of networking is to make as many connections as possible, not to stand around and socialize. Think of your time at these functions as if it were money. You can't afford to stand around with one person for too long. After about eight minutes with one person tell that person you are pleased to have met him or her and move on. If there is someone you seem to be getting along with really well, instead of chatting for a long time or sitting next to him or her for dinner, invite that person out to lunch.

Most likely your memory will not retain information on every person you meet. Collect business cards and write down physical features of the people you meet along with subjects you discussed to help you remember them the next time you see them. Review these cards when you go to another networking session for the same group. Likewise, hand out your business cards as much as possible, but don't make it seem as though you are dealing out a deck of cards. Be subtle and make giving each card meaningful. When someone hands you a business card study it and look at the person who handed it to you. This not only shows respect, it will also help you remember who they are.

Networking as a host is the best way to get attention. There are a number of events you can host, and one of them is an educational seminar. Choose a topic that you are very knowledgeable in, and offer a hands-on workshop or a lecture (FREE is a good price). This is a good way to give people just enough information to pique their interest about what you do. Hopefully, they will contact you for more information and eventually become a customer.

Networking can also be done via the Internet. A listserv is an email mailing list. Several people interested in a certain subject sign up. Whenever a member sends a message to the list, everyone who signed up receives the message. Ask your local librarian to help you find a listserv directory, and look for listservs that suit your business interests. There are listservs specific to each industry, for women entrepreneurs, for small businesses, for salespeople, and anything else you can think of. Since members come from a wider geographic area, you are less likely to make contacts that can bring business to you. However, they can offer advice and you can learn from experiences of others.

Follow up with people you meet. Never wait for them to call you. Send them a written note about how you were glad to meet them, you hope to get to know them better, etc. They will be pleased that you took an interest in them. Always send a written thank-you note if they do a favor for you.

You may not be selling at these events, but networking can greatly enhance your knowledge and business. Fellow businesspeople are a rich resource for your success. Approach a networking situation an opportunity to share ideas and learn from others. Be generous with information and time. It will be paid back to you tenfold.

Questions

1.   What does networking mean to you?

2.   How can connections and networking benefit your business?

3.   What are three ways you can help people get what they want?

a)

b)

c)

4.   Name two people in your community whom you'd like to network with and explain why.

a)

b)

5.   What topics could you discuss with them?

6.   How can you learn about them before meeting with them?

7.   Do you consider yourself approachable? Why or why not?

8.   Write a short, simple message thanking a contact and expressing an interest in getting to know him or her better.

_____

_____

_____

Answers

1. Imagine you are joining a group of fellow entrepreneurs. What do you hope to get out of it?

2. Describe what a network of fellow entrepreneurs can do for your business. Be specific.

3. One possibility is to offer them a free service. This could be an exchange of services. Or it could be free with no obligations. Later, if you need a favor from them, they will remember your generosity.

4. Think about specific people or businesses that will benefit you and your business. Usually they will be in the same line of work or in a related field. Or, they might have a lot of power or have a lot of connections from which you could benefit.

5. After you decide who you'd like to know, think of some topics you can discuss to establish rapport. What do you know about their interests and hobbies?

6. Think of some ways you can learn about them. Do you know one of their friends? Would it be appropriate to call an assistant or co-worker to chat?

7. Look at yourself in the mirror. Would you approach someone like yourself? Think about what would hold you back. You could be put off by nervous ticks, an unsmiling face, out of style clothes, or a look of anxiety.

8. Keep it positive and focus on the benefits your contact will receive. Rehearse it.

20 - Promotional Products

What can promotional products do for your business?

There are hundreds of tools you can use to publicize your business. Promotional products are one of those tools. Promotional products get your name out there, remind customers of your business, and give people something for free. Salespeople and customers both gain from promotional products.

The products can be distributed at trade shows, grand openings, special events, appointments, or in your office. Everybody likes free merchandise. When you hand them a free product, you make a connection, start a conversation, and perhaps eventually make a sale. Promotional products can oftentimes provide the link needed to begin establishing rapport. People open up more when you give them something for nothing.

However, never make receiving of a free promotional product a condition of listening to your sales pitch. If people seem responsive or ask you questions, go for it. However, giving them a sales pitch they don't want to hear while they're choosing a refrigerator magnet will make it seem as if magnet selection is more trouble than it's worth.

And why would you want them to have a refrigerator magnet? Because when friends come over to visit they will see the magnet while their host is getting them a drink. Because when a friend asks if they know someone who sells such and such a product, they will remember the magnet. Because they will put the magnet in the free box at their garage sale and someone else will put it on their refrigerator.

Besides increasing your visibility, receiving free products makes people feel good. And that's your goal, to try to create good feelings in customers and potential customers. Recently, I received a $15 gift card from an office supply store. The only obligation was that I had to make a minimum purchase of $15. First, I was surprised to receive it. I reread the letter that came with it to look for the small type that would reveal the catch, but there was none. My overall impression of the public relations move was that it was very generous. I left with a smile on my face and a good opinion of the store because they gave me something and expected nothing back.

Promotional products can also serve to announce a new product or service or a change in your product or service. When marketing through the mail however, your new announcement is likely to head straight to the wastebaskets. But if you enclose a pen, it will go into the top desk drawer.

Below are some other ideas from the book *101 Ways to Promote Your Business* for distributing promotional products:

* Employee incentives, awards, recognition programs
* Anniversary and birthday celebrations
* Holiday commemorations
* Direct-mail programs

- Thank you gifts
- Convention, conference, and trade show giveaways
- New product or service introductions
- Customer appreciation
- Corporate sales and staff meetings
- Sales campaigns
- Sponsored sports activities
- Relocation announcements
- Expansion announcements
- Travel and sales incentive gifts
- Hotel room amenities
- Travel gifts

Questions

1.   Discuss why promotional products are or are not useful to your particular business.

2.   Describe three effective promotional products you can use.

a)

b)

c)

3.   Describe three ways that you can distribute promotional products.

a)

b)

c)

Answers

1.   Everybody likes something for nothing, but that doesn't necessarily mean it will be profitable to your business. Weigh the costs versus the benefits before deciding to hand out free items.

2.   Pens are an effective tool because they get passed around, lost, found, borrowed, maybe even crushed under a school bus and the janitor finds it and reads it.

3.   Probably the most popular way is to hand them out at trade shows.

NOTES:

21 - Written Communication

Why is it important that your letters be well written?

Remember the old days before email when people had to pick up a pen and write something on paper? Well, even though computers have virtually replaced pens, letters are still important in the business world. Business letters are usually sent to people outside the company, but they can be written for internal purposes as well. Most letters have a formal tone. Expectations for written communication are much higher than they are for email. You still need to know how to compose a well-written letter and communicate your points effectively. A poorly written letter will add nothing to your image. A well-written letter demonstrates that you are a professional company that pays attention to the details of how you conduct business. This chapter will provide some basic tips on written communication.

There are many reasons to write business letters. They can provide someone with specific information. They might persuade someone to take action. They can propose an idea, sell a product or service, or say thank you. In sales, a letter can serve to protect both you and your customer. The document can serve as a contract: a written record of the terms of your agreement. Business letters can be difficult to write because you have to keep your reader's attention. If you are selling something, you are competing with several other companies that send the same kinds of letter.

Think about your audience. Usually your audience is other professionals. Sometimes it is customers or prospective customers. The audience may even be your co-workers. The tone of your letter will depend on the make-up of your audience, but always make it polite and positive.

The next step is to determine the purpose of your letter. You should to get to the point quickly, clearly, and accurately. Any written communication should be typed and printed on company letterhead. Write the way you speak. There is no need to make it an academic paper.

Remember that a business letter reflects your level of professionalism. The words you choose, your grammar, and spelling all reflect on the company, and your ability to get it right when you provide a product or service.

All business letterheads should include the name of your company, a return address, and a phone number. The date comes next. Use the date the letter was finished. It should be two inches from the top of the page and aligned left or centered. Next, include the address of the person to whom you are writing. This should be one inch below the date and aligned left. Two lines below the recipient's address comes the salutation. It is always best to write to a specific person and include a personal title such as Ms., Mrs., Mr., Dean, or Dr. If you know the person, it is acceptable to address the person by his or her first name. The standard way to punctuate a salutation is with a colon.

The body of the letter should be single-spaced and aligned left. Leave a blank line between each paragraph. Begin with a friendly opening, and then in the same paragraph, briefly state your purpose for writing. The second paragraph should go into more detail about your purpose. This might include background information, statistics, or an example. In the closing paragraph, briefly summarize your purpose, thank the reader for his or her time, and if appropriate, include contact information. The sign-off should be one line after the last paragraph and aligned left. Then leave four lines for the sender's signature and type out the sender's name. "Sincerely" is the most common way to close a letter.

In sales, you want to write a letter that initiates some form of action. There are three components to an action-oriented letter. The first is stating what action you want your readers to take. Should they order your product or service? Should they visit your store for a tour or demo? Should they set up an appointment? Fill out a form? Tell them exactly what you want them to do and how to do it.

Then, tell readers the benefits for taking action. Let readers know what they will gain by taking prompt action. Lastly, set a date. Tell readers by what date they need to take action. Diplomatically tell them why you need them to take action by that date. Throughout your letter, use active verbs that stir people's emotions. Remember "you" and "your" will have more impact than "I" and "we."

Writing is all about your image. Just as you convey your level of professionalism in the way you dress, shake hands, use body language, and speak; you also convey professionalism in your written communication. Think about your audience, your purpose, and your choice of words when you write. Make it neat. Spell check *and* proofread everything you write. Your writing is an opportunity to win over customers and form strong relationships.

Questions

1. Write a sample letter to a customer thanking him or her for purchasing your product or using your service. Use the guidelines in this chapter. The letter should be about three paragraphs.

2.	Now write a sales letter urging the customer to take some form of action. It should be about three paragraphs.

Answers

1.

October 23, 2004

Mary Smith

451 Orange Street

Anytown, USA 90000

Dear Ms. Smith:

Congratulations on the purchase of your new car. I would like to take this opportunity to thank you for choosing Monson Motors for your automotive needs. Monson Motors is honored to have customers like you.

I know you will be pleased with your new car. Monson Motors makes every effort to keep our customers happy.

I hope you will keep us in mind for your future needs. If there is anything we can do for you to help you adjust to your new car, please let us know. We are happy to serve you.

Sincerely,

Tom Monson

2.

Do great salespeople make more money?

If you are like most people, you want to make more money. If I could show you how to make more money each day, would you be willing to invest in just a few hours of training?

Why be content to just get by when you can increase your profit by building a powerful and knowledgeable sales force? Great salespeople know what customers want. They know the meaning of great customer service and how it translates into profit. They know how to make the sale!

Now you can too…

You'll be pleased to know there is a sales training course right here in Anytown. "Smart Selling: How to Understand Your Customers" is a 4-hour program that makes the sales process clear and easy to understand. The program is divided into three sections:

1) **Building strong relationships with customers** — Salespeople will learn how to establish rapport and build trust with customers and clients.

2) **Focusing on a customer's needs** — Salespeople will learn how to ask questions to determine customers' needs and match products or services to those needs.

3) **Dealing with objections and closing the sale** — Salespeople will learn the best ways to handle customers' objections. They will also learn how to close a sale effectively.

This program will build a confident and motivated sales force. Everyone in your company can benefit from sales training that focuses on customer service. Register your salespeople for "Smart Selling: How to Understand Your Customers." With just 4 hours of training, your salespeople will be selling like they never sold before.

We are so confident that your sales will increase that we offer a money back satisfaction guarantee. Simply call Advantage Source today at 541-779-0016 and get your sales team on the right track!

Sincerely,

Tom Monson

P.S. Did you know that for every dollar invested in training there is a $100 return in profit?

22 - Brochures

Why are brochures important for a company?

A brochure is another effective tool for promoting your business. Brochures are meant to pique interest and to be informational. They can answer questions your customers might have or they can let customers know more about you.

A brochure can help initiate conversation between a salesperson and a prospect. It might be a good idea to send prospects brochures and informational materials before you meet with them. This allows them time to learn more about you and your product or service and formulate questions. Some customers don't like to be given information without the chance to think it over and respond to it.

There are two philosophies concerning brochures. One is that the brochure provides basic information to get customers interested. Then you can expand on the brochure by speaking to them in person. The other strategy is to design brochure that tries to answer any anticipated questions by giving detailed information. There is no right answer. It may depend on the nature of your business. If you spend a lot of time with customers and clients, you don't need a brochure that says too much. You can send a brochure that gives some basic information on a new product, for example, and then follow up with a phone call or visit. Brochures with lots of information are good for people who call you but can't meet with you in person.

A well-crafted brochure can even raise your image above that of the competition. A black and white brochure on flimsy paper with low quality photos doesn't stand a chance against a four-color brochure on stiff, glossy paper. Your company will appear more professional and more credible. The quality of your brochure will reflect the quality of your business. A cheap brochure contributes to an image of inferior, low quality service or products.

A brochure should ask customers to do something – call for an appointment, request more information, or ask for an order.

The brochure should have the prospect in mind. This is not an opportunity to brag about yourself and your accomplishments. You can include testimonials, but never overload your brochure with one testimonial after another. Make sure your testimonials show the reader how the customer benefited from using your product or service. For the most part, you simply want to inform readers, rally them to your cause, and make a sale. Those are your primary goals.

A brochure that is sent out in the mail should contain general information about products. The letter that accompanies the brochure should be written using sales language. Use the language of your industry in your writing, unless you are trying to appeal to mass audiences. Otherwise, you will look like an outsider in your own industry. Avoid using big, fancy words. Your brochure will be ineffective if people can't understand it.

Brochures must speak to people. Reading a brochure that simply lists the products available, describes them, and gives their cost is more like reading a term paper than an advertising piece. The brochure should focus on what your product or service can do for people. How can you make their lives easier? How will they benefit?

Too much information could be overwhelming. Many brochures created merely to pique attention contain so much information they are intimidating. You can break up information to make it more readable by using bullets, numbers, and boxes.

Graphics and photos can be a blessing or a curse. If you are not a graphic designer, don't pretend to be one. A professionally created brochure will payoff in terms of your company's image. Visualize what the brochure will look like on a display rack. Does yours stand out? Would you pick it up if you had a casual interest? Never use those cheap computer programs that provide templates either. Many people have these programs themselves and will know the templates. It will make your company look cheap.

Keep your brochures current. The last thing you want is to have customers make a decision based on outdated information. It is bad for your image to have to inform them that something stated in your brochure is no longer correct or that a certain product is no longer available. And it is *really* bad to have to inform them that the price has changed. Most brochures should be updated at least once a year. Never cross out dated information. This looks unprofessional. Leave prices out of most brochures. Allow customers to have a reason to call and ask questions.

Always include contact information on your brochure, preferably on the front cover. This is a basic part of advertising, yet it is sometimes overlooked.

You can also build a sales presentation around a brochure. This is accomplished when you study the brochure and use it to show benefits to the customer. Use your brochures as a tool to sell, not as the end all to selling. Decide what you want your brochure to accomplish and how it will be used before you create it. Sometimes a brochure is used when there is a better way to accomplish the task.

Here are some questions for you to ask before creating a brochure:

- Who is your audience and what do you want them to think and feel after viewing your brochure?

- What are you trying to accomplish with a brochure in terms of your marketing strategy?

- How will the brochure be coordinated with other marketing tools?

- How will the brochure be distributed to customers?

- What is the most important message(s) you want to get out to your customers?

Keep your brochure simple and uncluttered. Have more white space than ink. Don't try to do too much. Be different but don't try to be eccentric. It could backfire. If you can afford it, a full color brochure is usually the most attractive. Stress quality and benefits to the customer in your brochure.

Questions

1.   Who is the audience for your brochure?

2.   What do you want your brochure to accomplish?

3.   What does your brochure ask customers to do?

4.   Do testimonials in your brochure convey how customers benefited from your product or service? Give an example.

5.   How often do you update your brochures? Is this sufficient?

Answers

1.   The audience may be customers, other vendors, members of the public, members of your congregation, etc. The audience may be more specific: women, Native Americans, Jews, veterans, etc. Think even more specifically. The audience could be abused women, Native Americans with a college degree, Jews who enjoy baseball, or veterans needing medical care.

2.   Depending on your business or organization, a brochure can be primarily informational. It can be meant to inspire. Or it may be a call to action.

3.   This only applies if your brochure is a call to action. You have to state specifically what you want customers to do.

4.   Examine the content of your testimonials. If they do not indicate a benefit, find some that do.

5.   This will be different for every business and will depend on the type of information contained in your brochures. Remember, styles change and your brochure should reflect what is in style today.

NOTES:

_____

_____

_____

_____

_____

_____

_____

_____

_____

_____

_____

_____

_____

_____

_____

_____

_____

_____

_____

_____

23 - Remember Names

How do you feel when people remember your name?

Aren't you impressed when you run into people you met weeks ago and they greet you by saying your name? Is it that they have a photographic memory and never forget a name or face? Possibly, but it might also be that they have a genuine interest in people. Or like me, they made an extra effort to implant your name in their mind.

You may say, "I'm not good at remembering names." Well, stop right there. Your subconscious mind (which does whatever you tell it to) will obey and make that statement come true. If you think you can't remember names, stop telling yourself you can't remember names. Come up with a different story because when you start remembering people's names is when you will become much more successful than you are right now. Guaranteed!

Remembering a person's name can earn you many points in sales and in networking circles. It makes people feel important. It makes them think you care about them. It lets them know you are meeting people because you like people and not just because you need acquaintances to get ahead.

Everybody loves the sound of their own name. Making a little extra effort to remember someone's name may not be as hard as you think. When introduced to someone, repeat that person's name two to four times in a conversation. For example, you can say, "It's nice to meet you, Jane," or "So Jane, what do you do for a living?" or "What outdoor activities do you enjoy, Jane?"

You can also try to associate her name with an interest, physical feature, or someone else you know. Does she have the same name as your aunt? Is he tall and does he have the same name as a great basketball player you admire? If her name is Lucy, does she have red hair like your favorite comedian from the 1950s?

After you leave the conversation and when you are alone, you can write down the name and a description of the person to keep for future reference. We are much more likely to remember things when we write them down.

Just because you have taken pains to remember another person's name doesn't mean he or she is as astute as you are. If you meet somebody you haven't seen for a long time, chances are that person has forgotten your name. This often leads to an awkward situation in which that person apologizes for forgetting your name. You can prevent him or her from embarrassment by reminding that person of who you are, while at the same time, remembering his or her name. For example, "Hello, Jane. It's nice to see you again. I'm Toni."

Keep in mind that everybody's name is important to them regardless of whether they are a prospect, a gatekeeper, the gatekeeper's second cousin, his dog, or a multimillion dollar customer. Remembering a name is all part of the "Becoming-Genuinely-Interested-in-Other-People" package. You will find that a little effort goes a long way toward making a good impression.

Questions

1.   How does it feel when a casual acquaintance remembers your name?

2.   How are you at remembering names?

3.   Do you have a strategy for remembering a name? Explain it.

4.   What would be appropriate to say to someone whose name you have forgotten?

5.   What can you say to someone who has forgotten your name so that the person doesn't feel embarrassed?

Answers

1. Most people like it when you remember their name. It makes them feel important.

2. Rate yourself on a scale of one to ten where ten is the best. Do you seem to remember some names better than others? Explain.

3. One person's strategy was to think of a famous person with the same name as the one she just heard.

4. You can say something like, "I'm sorry, I've met so many people today. Please tell me your name again..."

5. "Just in case you don't remember, my name is Sarah..."

24 - Keep a Profile for Prospects and Contacts

Why would you want to keep a profile on each customer?

Establishing rapport with customers is a process that evolves over time. Your first meeting is the most important one for establishing rapport, but maintaining that rapport for weeks and years to come is also important. You want to build a long-term relationship with customers so that they see you as more than just a vendor. A strong relationship produces loyalty, which will endure hard times and any mistakes you may make along the way.

One way to build rapport over time is to keep a profile sheet on each customer and anyone associated with that customer. The more information you can gather about the customer, the better. Information should be divided into two categories: business-related and personal. Of course you want to find out what's important to him or her in terms of the company's needs and goals, but equally vital is what's important in his or her personal life.

After you meet with customers, write down anything about their personal life they may have mentioned. Note things like birthdays, spouses, children, grandchildren, hobbies, personal goals, where they like to vacation, pets, favorite movies, TV shows, books, sports teams, athletes they admire, etc. Send birthday and holiday cards. If you see an article about their child in the newspaper, clip it out and send it to the customers. They will be pleased you noticed.

Do not ask questions as though you are collecting data to write a biography on them. Introduce the questions as part of casual conversation. If you feel as if you are not getting enough information, let them know your interests first and then they may be more eager to share their interests. However, do not go into great detail about yourself. A movie or book synopsis is especially boring for most people. Let them do most of the talking. The more you ask, the more you know.

Jot down any information about a customer offered by gatekeepers or other people who know the customer. Ask them questions as well. Later you can engage the customer with something like, "I heard you used to play football in high school."

Review your profiles every month. You never know when you are going to run into a contact or customer. If you know you are going to see a contact, review the contact's profile before you meet with him or her. Ask about his or her kids by name. Ask how that old mutt is doing. Ask how many fish were caught on that fishing trip he or she was talking about last time you saw him or her. The customer will be impressed by your memory, and you will be developing a more relaxed atmosphere, putting the customer at ease.

Questions

1. How do you feel when people ask about something that is important to you personally?

2. Design a method for recording information on prospects and customers.

3. What types of information will you collect?

4. How will you use this information in the future?

Answers

1. Most people would feel flattered that someone paid attention to what they find interesting.

2. Probably the most popular method is to keep a card file.

3. Each card lists any information that you can gather about the customer. If you work in a dentist's office and a patient mentions that his dog got hit by a car, write that down on the chart and ask how the dog is doing next time he comes in. Make sure you write down that you asked him or her how the dog was doing. Otherwise, you might ask again and he or she will think you weren't paying attention the first time.

4. Review each customer's file before meeting with him or her.

25 - Cold Calling

What is the key to a successful cold call?

Cold calling by phone is probably the quickest and most cost-effective way to generate business. Your effectiveness depends on your approach to cold calling. A successful approach involves preparation, quick thinking, perseverance, and fearlessness. You are at a disadvantage at the beginning of the call because the recipient is automatically put on the defensive. You have interrupted the person and made him or her switch gears to listen to you.

Preparation is the key to succeeding in a cold call. Write a script of what you will say as often as possible. The way you word your questions will have a significant impact on how successful you will be making cold calls. If you have to deal with gatekeepers, your first objective is to get him or her to connect you to the person with whom you wish to speak. Ask the gatekeeper a question like, "What is the name of the person who makes decisions regarding…?" Then, ask to speak to that person.

Many times the gatekeeper will ask for more information about you. Try to answer in the form of a question. For example, when asked for your name, say something like, "Will you tell him or her my name is Tom Monson from Salchow Skates?" Never mislead a gatekeeper or the prospect about who you are, where you are from, and why you are calling. They will resent you when they find out the truth and you will never be able to get past them again.

Most people you call may start out on the defensive because they feel trapped on the phone. They've lost control. You are interrupting their workday. They have to switch from what they were working on to listen to you. Try to build rapport by asking them about something unrelated to the sale. You will learn a lot about them by how they answer. The tone of their voice will tell you how you need to proceed. If they seem friendly, continue establishing rapport. If they seem annoyed or impatient, get to the point of your call quickly. Try to mirror the prospect's speed and tone of voice.

Prepare exactly what you are going to say ahead of time. To script or not to script? It is your choice if you want to work from a script. Scripts can help you stay on track and keep you from getting tongue-tied. However, scripts can also make you sound like you're reading.

Think about the goal of the cold call. What are you trying to do? Make a sale? Get an appointment? Either way, you have to establish enough rapport to get your prospect to listen to you. Once you get the right person on the phone, you want to give him or her a reason to listen to you. Get permission to talk first. Ask something like, "I know you are busy right now and this may not be a good time. When would be the best time for me to call back?" Often, they will be willing to take the time right then.

If you are making a call to someone you were referred to, do some research on the person. Then you can say something like, "So-and-so suggested I contact you. I understand you supply oxygen to patients. There's a new kind of oxygen that can be carried in a backpack or on a belt instead of wheeled around. I would like to tell you how this new system can make people's lives easier and give them more freedom."

One effective way to reach the right person is to send a letter first. State that you will follow up with a phone call in a few days. Then tell the gatekeeper that so and so is expecting your call.

Unless you are strictly a telemarketer, your main objective is to make an appointment. People prefer appointments. Appointments save time for both the salespeople and the customer. Time becomes a commodity when an appointment is made. What takes place in an arranged meeting is taken more seriously than what happens when you just stop by. The customer agreed to make time for you in his or her schedule and will be more receptive to what you have to say.

Before you meet with prospects, let them know what you will cover in the meeting. You might want to send some literature in advance, but never do this unless they seem genuinely interested. Unsolicited mail almost always gets thrown away. Send an "agenda" of what you will talk about. So that the prospect doesn't think you are coming in to bombard him or her with high-pressure sales tactics, mention that there is no obligation to buy. You can also offer a guarantee or a free trial period.

Every time you leave a cold call or an appointment, ask the customer if he or she knows of anybody else in the area who could benefit from your product or service. When you get a referral, act quickly. The longer you set aside a referral, the more you lose the motivation to follow through on it.

Are you a procrastinator? Procrastination is usually based on fear of failure and rejection. Almost all fears can be overcome. The best strategy is to do the very thing you are afraid of. You can overcome your fear of cold calling by making more cold calls. Begin by setting a goal for how many cold calls you'll do each day.

Gradually increase the number of calls you do each day. You'll get better at making calls so they will go faster. Over time, you'll realize that the negative things you thought would happen either never actually happen or you are capable of dealing with them.

Keep track of your results. Log each call and note what transpired. You will be able to go back and look at how your effort contributes to your results. Lastly, there must be somebody to whom you are held accountable. You need to report weekly progress to this person. This may all sound like basic advice, but these methods are tried and true. They have worked for millions of salespeople, and they will work for you too.

Remember if you look at your actions and not the results, you will go much farther.

When you make the call you have to remember you are on stage and the prospect will mirror you and how you present yourself. If you are up and personable you will have a much better chance of getting somewhere with him than if you projected your attitude about hating making cold calls.

There is some great information in the book *Never Cold Call Again,* Frank Rumbauskas. He shows salespeople how to achieve sales greatness without using those dreaded old tactics like cold calling. He gives small business owners, independent professionals, and entrepreneurs a complete, all-in-one guide to the best practices of effective online marketing.

Questions

1. Write a rough draft of a script you can use to make cold calls. This script should apply to cold calling both by phone and in person. Even if you don't stick to the script, you should write out what you will say in advance.

2. Think about three possible problems you may encounter, and write down specifically how you will deal with those problems.

a)

b)

c)

Answers

1. Here is a sample script. Your only objective is to gain an appointment with this prospect. This assumes that you know the name of the person you are calling. Pretend it's a friend you haven't seen for many years.

You: Hello, This is Monson, Tom Monson, is this Mr. Jones?

Mr. Jones: Yes.

You: Did I catch you at a good time?

Mr. Jones: What can I do for you?

You: Thanks, Mr. Jones, please call me Tom, I'm with XYZ Insurance here in LA. and Oh my gosh, did you see the Dodger game last night?

(This is where you should try to establish some type of rapport with your prospect. You can ask something about the weather, local sports or anything that you share a common interest in. His or her reply will also tell you a lot about the kind of person he or she is.)

Mr. Jones: Listen, I don't have time to talk about the Dodgers, especially with an insurance agent.

You: I can certainly appreciate that so I will be brief. If you have a moment, I would like to offer you a free review of your coverage and any liabilities that may not be covered. I was wondering when would be the best time to take a look. It should only take a few minutes. Would later this week be good or would early next week be better?

(Wait for a response.)

Mr. Jones: I really have all the insurance I need and I already have a retirement program. I don't think I need anything right now.

You: I realize that talking to me about insurance right now may not create a lot of enthusiasm on your part. Could I ask you one question?

Mr. Jones: I'm really running out of time here so make it quick.

You: Great, thank you. Here's the question: If I could show you a way to increase your coverage and reduce your premiums, would you be willing to sit down with me for about 10 minutes to take a look at a very competitive program?

(Wait for response.)

Mr. Jones: As long as it doesn't take any longer than that.

You: Okay, I'll make it short.

So you make arrangements to meet with her and provide all the good stuff you provide. When you make friends with your potential customer, you will be on your way.

2.　　　　Possible problems might be:

- Getting past the gatekeeper

- Getting to the person who makes decisions

- Dealing with someone who doesn't have time for you

- Getting through to a person who won't return your calls

- Hearing he or she tell you they hate telemarketers

- Hearing he or she tell you to just send some brochures

26 - Gatekeepers

Why should you be nice to gatekeepers?

Whether cold calling or arriving for an appointment, the gatekeeper (an assistant or secretary) can be your biggest ally or your worst opponent. You should be nice to gatekeepers. Often they will have more power than you think. They may make some important decisions themselves or be able to influence the people who do make the decisions. In any case, they can be a great source of information that can help you establish rapport with potential clients.

Treat gatekeepers the same way you treat prospects. You are much more likely to get what you want if you show them respect. They are as important as you and the person you want to speak with. Form a relationship with them the same way you do with your prospects. Remember their names. Remember their children's names. Remember what kind of dog they have. Find out about their likes and dislikes, their hobbies, and keep a written profile on them. Become genuinely interested in them first. Then you can ask them about the prospect's interests and hobbies.

If you are able to establish this kind of relationship with gatekeepers, they are more likely to spread the word about your product or service or use it themselves. They will probably not remember all the advantages of your product or service, but they will remember the friendly salesperson.

If a gatekeeper seemed particularly helpful, you can show your appreciation by sending a thank you note. Include some kind of compliment related to a job well done and make it specific. Indicate that you look forward to seeing him or her again.

Many administrative assistants are taught how to weed out telephone and face-to-face solicitors. If you are cold calling, the challenge for you is getting through the gatekeeper in order to set up an appointment to meet with the person who makes buying decisions.

When cold calling, introduce yourself and the company you represent. Gatekeepers and prospects do not like salespeople who mislead them about who they are, whom they represent, and what they are there for. They resent salespeople who use deception to get through the door. They prefer a sincere, honest, and straightforward approach.

Ask the gatekeeper if the owner is in or for the name of the president of the company. Then ask about the best way to contact him or her. You can also ask for the person who makes the purchasing decisions. Start with the head of the company and work your way down.

Once you get through the gatekeeper, you may still not be speaking to the person who has the authority to make purchasing decisions. Two questions to help you determine who has purchasing power are:

- Should we involve anyone else in the meeting in order to make a decision about this product or service?

- What is the process for making buying decisions in your company?

Gatekeepers might seem like an obstacle you must cleverly plot your course around, but remember that they can be your lifeline. Show the gatekeepers you respect them and care as much about them as you do the potential client. Most of the time you will receive that respect in return.

Questions

1.   Describe an effective way to approach gatekeepers.

2.   What could you do to form a close bond with a gatekeeper?

3.   Write down everything you think you should know about a gatekeeper to carry on a conversation with him or her.

4.   How can a gatekeeper help you make a sale?

5.   Think of three ways you can show a gatekeeper you appreciate his or her help.

a)

b)

c)

6.   When cold calling, how would you handle a gatekeeper who seems resistant to letting you meet with a prospective client?

Answers

1.   Try two or three different ways of approaching a gatekeeper. Describe which one worked the best and why. What were your first words?

2.   Describe how you will establish rapport.

3.   Find out the gatekeeper's name, job responsibilities, what he or she likes about the job, information about family, hobbies, etc.

4.   Think of what information or power gatekeepers might have that would contribute to their employer deciding to purchase your product or service.

5.   List a few things you could give to a gatekeeper, like a thank you card or a gift.

6.   Write down exactly what you would say and the body language and/or behaviors you'd use.

NOTES:

_____

_____

_____

_____

_____

_____

_____

_____

_____

_____

_____

_____

_____

_____

_____

_____

_____

_____

_____

_____

_____

_____

27 - Research Prospective Customers

What do you need to know before meeting with a prospect?

You show up for a meeting with a prospect. After the initial greeting the prospect sits down and asks you, "So why did you choose *me* to come talk to today?" What do you say? How can you sincerely show prospects that you are interested specifically in them and their business? For one thing, you can do some research so that you can come up with a reason why you are there to see that particular prospect. Perhaps you will discover an area where the company is falling short and your product or service can fill the gap.

Now the issues become what and how do you research. The following information will prove beneficial when meeting with a client:

- Company history and background information

- Mission statement and goals

- What products it manufactures or services it offers

- Who its customers are, what the customers want, and how the company serves them

- Its employees and what makes them most productive

- Who its competitors are and how its business is doing relative to the competition

- Budget and spending priorities

Some of this information will be easy to find. Collect and read brochures, newsletters, annual reports, and web pages. Use people to help you as well. If you know any of the company's customers, talk to them. Ask them what they like about the company's products and services as well as what they would like the company to improve on. Gatekeepers can also be a valuable source of information. Always be nice to whomever answers the phone because you never know who it is and how they are to help you. Gatekeepers can be your source for collecting literature, but they can also tell you about the prospects' hobbies, interests, and personality traits that will help you to establish rapport.

Another way to collect information is by attending trade shows. Trade shows provide a wealth of company literature. They also allow you to learn about competitors and to talk to people in the industry.

Other types of information that require more searching but are invaluable sources of information are newspaper articles, press releases, and journal and magazine articles. There may even be a book written about or authored by the company. Librarians can teach you more sophisticated research methods for Internet and electronic database literature searches.

Other information can only be gathered by asking the prospect direct, open-ended questions. There is a list of questions in the chapter entitled, "Qualifying the Customer." Don't be afraid to probe prospects for specific information. The more you know about specific problems they are having or areas they would like to improve on, the more specific your solution can be.

Researching a company may seem time-consuming and difficult, but it will pay off when you meet with the prospect. Customers will be pleased that you have gone out of your way to learn about them; and you will be seen as someone who is prepared, conscientious, and hard-working. They will know that if you work hard before a sale you will also work hard during and after a sale.

Questions

1.   Make a list of what you should know about a customer before meeting with him or her.

2.   How will you find this information?

3.   How will you make sure you know this information when you get to the meeting?

Answers

1.   Some things might include: the number of employees, who the customers are, how the company has evolved over time, etc. Think of more things that are specific to your type of business.

2.   Devise a strategy for research. Think of people who can help and what types of information you will pursue.

3.   Describe your study habits. Will you write the information down? Will you memorize it? Test yourself? Role play?

NOTES:

28 - Qualify Your Customers

What should you do before you begin a sales pitch?

It is more important to understand what your customers need and want than to try to convince them to buy what you have. Salespeople are sometimes so eager to make a sale that they try to manipulate a customer into thinking he or she needs their product or service rather than fit their product or service to the customer's needs. Instead of beginning your sales pitch by touting all the great features of your product or service, find out what the customer needs first. It doesn't matter how great the product is if he or she doesn't need it. Ask questions to determine if customers actually have a need for your product or service. Then find out if they are ready to buy, if they have the money to buy, and if they have the authority to buy. Qualifying a customer takes skill but practice will produce results. Below is a list of sample questions to help you pinpoint what customers need.

Questions to ask customers:

- What are you doing now in terms of this type of product or service? Try to find out about other vendors they are using and how they are working for them. Ask about any problems they are having or what they would like to have that they are not currently getting.

- How long have you been in business? Your sales approach may differ depending on the longevity of your customers' experience.

- Why did you switch vendors? If they are switching to you from another vendor or if they have told you that they are looking for a new vendor, ask them why.

- May I ask what you are paying your vendor? This will help you to be competitive and to determine how much they can afford if they switch to your company.

- Is there anyone besides yourself who is responsible for making purchasing decisions? Find out if the person to whom you are speaking has the authority to make buying decisions.

- What are the challenges your business is facing today? You always want to be thinking about their problems and how you can solve them.

- What are your company's goals for the next year? Five years? Ten years? Anticipate their needs.

- What do you look for when you choose a new vendor? Knowing what they like will help you serve them better.

- What are your expectations for service and product quality? Ask yourself if your product or service can live up to their expectations.

- What would you change about your present vendor's product or service? This will tell you what they are unhappy about. Be careful not to join in if they begin bad-mouthing a vendor. Just take notes.

- Can you tell me about how much you are looking to invest in this product or service? You may need to explain to the customer that sometimes investing less now will cost more later.

- What is your time frame for making this buying decision? You don't want to waste your time if they aren't prepared to buy for another five years.

- Do you have a timeline? A timeline is a specific set of dates for when the different steps of a project should be completed. This will give you an idea of whether or not you can deliver on schedule.

- How is your company different from the competition? You may have a product or service that can help them rise above the others.

- What do your customers say about your product or service? If customers are complaining about a problem, you might be able to help them out by offering suggestions on how to help their customers.

- How can I provide support after the sale is made? The customer will be impressed that you are not there merely to make a sale. You will learn how to take care of them on a long-term basis.

- Do you have a way to evaluate the service your vendors provide? They may not necessarily know they are getting bad service. An evaluation plan helps them think about what they might be lacking.

Don't overwhelm potential customers with a never-ending list of questions. Ask about seven questions that apply to their company and zero in on what you need to know. Make your questions direct. Never beat around the bush. Talk with more than one person if possible. An employee may give you a different perspective than the boss would give. Never jump to conclusions. Be patient and hear what each person has to say. Ask follow up questions.

If you conclude that you are not the vendor who is best-suited to fulfill your potential customer's needs after you have qualified him or her, it is best to be honest about it. You never want to gain a bad reputation for insisting your product or service will meet someone's needs when in fact it is virtually useless to him or her. Recommend someone you think can better serve them. Try to establish a partnership with a competitor (one of your networking connections) to send customers to one another when you are unable to help them. Let the potential customer know you are available to help in the future.

Questions

1. Make a list of ten questions you will ask your customer in order to sell your product or service. You should ask only about 7-8 questions, but you should have a couple of extras prepared.

1. _____

2. _____

3. _____

4. _____

5. _____

6. _____

7. _____

8. _____

9. _____

10. _____

2. What will you do if it seems as if your company is not the vendor who is best-suited to meet a customer's needs?

Answers

1. These questions should be about what your customer needs. Some may be broad such as, "What kind of car are you looking for?" Others may be more specific such as, "What color would you like?"

2. This is where you have to examine how much you want the sale. Some salespeople would try to sell them something anyway. Other salespeople would try to direct the customer to someone who could meet his or her needs more effectively.

Successful Selling

29 - Establish Rapport

What is the number one factor that influences the decision to buy?

If prospects agree to meet with you, chances are they are interested in your product. Sounds good, right? Not necessarily. You may be competing with several other vendors. What makes you so special? Perhaps you have the best deal. Maybe your customers can get the biggest bang for their buck by choosing you. But surveys show that price is only fourth on the list of reasons why people choose to buy from a particular vendor.

The number one reason for buying has to do with the confidence people have in the salesperson or company with which they are dealing. People buy when they feel good about you. When you first meet prospects, there is no reason for them to have any confidence in you. You are probably just another salesperson. It is your job to get to know them and earn their trust.

If you simply launch into your sales pitch and describe the great features of your products, you have missed the most important part of making a sale – establishing rapport with your potential customer. You have to sell yourself first. This doesn't mean reciting your résumé and all your accomplishments. It means showing confidence and a positive attitude. It means taking the time to get to know people. This process begins with your handshake and continues throughout the business relationship.

How do you win people's confidence? By showing a genuine interest in them. If you are not a people person, if you are not fascinated by the stories people tell, if you don't like to sit around and chat for a while, you are in the wrong line of work. A salesperson has to want to get to know people. A salesperson likes to ask questions. Salespeople love to listen. They know how to make people feel important. They know how to put people at ease. Salespeople look around an office and use the surroundings as a springboard for stimulating conversation.

The first thing to do is encourage people to talk about themselves. Most people like to do this anyway, but with your encouragement, they can really let themselves go. Meanwhile, you are absorbed in what they are saying. Let them do most of the talking and try not to interrupt. Never interject with your own stories and ideas. They don't care about your summer vacation. They want to brag about their own. You can make far more friends by being interested in other people than by getting people to be interested in you. Let them have the stage. Admire your customers' achievements. When they talk about their goals, never tell them how hard it will be to accomplish them. Support their ideas. Make them feel like the most important person in your life. You can't wait to hear everything they want to tell you.

Dale Carnegie says the greatest desire in human nature is to feel important. People will let you know in subtle ways what they want to be praised for. Listen to them attentively and you'll learn what is important to them. Find a way to compliment your customers, and make your compliments specific. Don't just say, "You look nice today." That sounds like a cliché. Instead, say, "I really like that new tie," or "You look great in blue," or "Where did you get those shoes? I've been wanting a pair just like them." If they have already used your products or services in the past, compliment them for something that has resulted from having used those products or services. This lets them realize the value of what you sell.

Avoid saying anything negative. The advice, "Say something nice or don't say anything at all" would apply here. Debate rages about the appropriateness of telling those little white lies ("Yes, Laura, I love your new haircut."). How can you possibly comment on a new haircut you don't like without hurting someone's feelings? In this case, a little flattery may be fine so long as it doesn't come across as fake or sarcastic. However, don't overdo it. Many people are perceptive enough to recognize insincerity and it can come back to haunt you.

Be careful with humor. If humor is not delivered gracefully, it loses its impact and can make the mood awkward rather than put someone at ease. People have different kinds of humor. Some love a humorous story that leads to a good belly laugh. Others like a very dry, sarcastic wit. Still others enjoy a joke with a great punch line. Not everyone appreciates the same kind of humor. You could be in hot water if you say something sarcastic and the other person thinks you are being disrespectful. A good rule of thumb is, don't attempt humor during your first few meetings. Observe what the other person's sense of humor is like and try to emulate it.

Do not bring up controversial topics like politics, religion, ethics, or the news. If the prospect brings up these topics and you disagree, don't say anything at all or a simple "yes" in agreement will suffice. If customers come to your place of business, avoid displaying religious or political icons, pictures, or signs where prospects can see them unless they are related to the nature of your business.

Similarly, do not try to offer advice on personal matters. If the prospect talks about personal problems early in the business relationship, you are not in a position to be counseling him or her. However, you can show empathy by listening. Most people simply want an empathetic ear. If they do ask you for advice, you can say something like, "I'm not sure I know enough about the situation to be very helpful, but I understand what you're saying and how you feel."

Likewise, never talk about your own problems. If they don't want to hear about your summer vacation, they certainly don't want to hear about your gallstones or your Aunt Gertrude's funeral. Make sure you leave your personal problems and your bad mood at the door. A prospect will not understand nor sympathize with your bad mood. Each customer deserves your positive and upbeat attitude.

There is much more to learn about the business of establishing rapport. Be sure to read the chapters on body language, remembering a name, positive attitude, being a good listener, and building trust.

Questions

1. Give an honest critique of how well you are able to establish rapport with people. It doesn't necessarily have to be in a sales environment. Do you make people feel comfortable? Are you able to carry on a conversation easily with people you just met?

2. What are three things you will work on to improve your ability to establish rapport?

a)

b)

c)

3. How much time do you think you need to establish rapport before trying to make a sale?

4. What are some controversial topics you should make a point of avoiding in your line of work?

5. How do you think a customer will perceive you if you talk about your personal problems?

Answers

1. The trick here is to be honest. Critique your social skills. How comfortable are you in both business and social situations?

2. Remember, you don't have to be an extrovert. You may just have to work at it a little more, but practice can make the difference. Write down specifically what you can practice.

3. This will depend on your level of comfort with people. You may need to try it a few times to get an idea of how other people respond to you.

4. These are usually political or religious. They may be personal issues as well, such as mental illnesses, family disputes, etc.

5. Think about how you'd react if you switched places and a salesperson started talking to you about his or her problems.

NOTES:

30 - Be Genuinely Interested in People

Why do people who show a genuine interest in others make more sales?

Can you tell the difference between people who speak to you just because they want you to buy something from them and people who speak to you because they have a genuine interest in you?

One of the themes throughout this book is sincerity. There may be many salespeople who can get away with flattery and a phony persona, but the salespeople who show a genuine interest in others are the ones who form long-term relationships and establish a fine reputation. If you are genuinely interested in people, you will be a great salesperson. If not, there is probably a job for you elsewhere.

It is hard to fake an interest in another person. Usually, listeners are so eager to share their own stories and experiences in a conversation that they are not really listening. This is revealed in the listener's facial expressions and body language. You know they are just dying to interject something they feel is more important than what you are saying. The advice in this situation is to zip it, unless you want to ask a question.

Being genuinely interested in people means you have to admit you have a lot to learn. You may listen to National Public Radio, watch PBS, or read *The New York Times*, but you really learn from other people. Even if you don't like what they are saying, there is always something to learn. If you can humble yourself enough to be open to the experiences of other people, you will find it easier to become genuinely interested in them.

When you show interest in other people, they will naturally be interested in you and what you have to say. Perhaps you recall a time when it seemed like someone rattled on and on about their ancestors, all the places they lived, how many children they had, where they all worked, who was notable for accomplishing what, and so forth. Then, he or she finally asked you about your ancestors and suddenly it was your turn to talk. It pays to listen. When you listen, people are more likely to ask you questions and then it is your turn to talk.

Your goal should be not to just sell a product, but to help people solve their problems. Showing a genuine interest in them will help establish the rapport you need to get people to open up and tell you their problem. Then, they will trust you to help them come up with a solution.

Think about the people you go to when you have a problem, either personal or professional. Ask yourself why you choose to go to them instead of someone else. Chances are they are warm, compassionate, sincere, and patient listeners. That is the kind of person you want to be.

Questions

1.   Think of someone (an acquaintance) who showed a genuine interest in you. What did he or she do to show an interest and how did you feel?

2.   Think of someone you regularly tell your problems to. What about him or her makes you choose that person?

3.   What are three things you will do to show a genuine interest in your customers?

a)

b)

c)

Answers

1. Most likely, he or she made you feel important. Did it make you want to listen to and believe in what he or she said?

2. What traits do you share with that person?

3. Think what the most important traits are for making people feel important. For example, being empathetic.

31 - Ask Questions

Why is it more important for salespeople to ask customers questions than speak to them?

The combination of being a good listener and asking questions is a critical strategy for establishing rapport and eventually making a sale. There are two different categories of questions to ask prospects and customers: one, questions that help you learn about your customer's needs; and two, more personal questions about family, hobbies, and interests that help you establish rapport with your customers. This chapter will deal with the first kind of question and why it is so important to ask rather than speak.

Some people feel as if they need to do all the talking because it helps them maintain control of the conversation. Never approach a sale as though you need to be in control. People don't like to be controlled, especially by a salesperson. Think about it this way. When you ask questions and listen to answers, you are gathering more information and knowledge about a problem or situation. The more questions you ask, the more information you will get, and the better you'll be able to help your customers. Only when people perceive you as willing to help them, can you begin showing them how your product or service will solve their problem.

Other salespeople never ask questions because they are afraid they might get a question in return that they won't be able to answer or won't want to answer. Instead, they deliver a speech on their product or service and think it went really well because the customer didn't say or ask anything. This is a bad sign. Quiet prospects are usually customers who feel threatened, alienated, or bored. If you are asked a question you can't answer, simply tell customers that you will find out the answer and let them know as soon as possible. If they ask a question that seems important to them and you can't answer it, then pick up the phone and call someone who knows. Your willingness to get an answer will be looked at favorably. If their question is one that doesn't seem important, write it down and tell them, "When we finish here, I'll get the answers to all of your questions." Of course this is much less likely to happen if you have done thorough research on your product or service.

Preface your question with "Let me ask you a question." This changes the way people respond to you. They become much more open and receptive to your question. This is because they switch from being defensive to being open-minded.

Ask open-ended questions. These are questions that require more than a yes, no, or one-word answer. This keeps the conversation going and allows you to learn more. It also makes prospects feel like they have some control of the situation. Asking questions also helps you find out how they feel about what is taking place. Listen for hesitation in their answers or excuses they make. Shy people don't always want to articulate their objections. They may just be trying to endure the sales pitch so they can give an insincere, "We'll let you know." Asking the right questions will draw out their real opinions.

If you feel yourself getting upset because of something that was said, start asking questions instead of saying something you may regret. Asking questions can help you avoid arguments. Your mind stays open when you ask questions because you are examining possibilities. When you are arguing your point your mind shuts down because your main focus is on showing someone else that you are right. You may win the argument but lose the sale.

If you are clever enough, asking questions can make other people think your idea is actually their idea. You can lead people to your conclusion by asking questions in such a way that they come up with the answer on their own. This is called the Socratic Method, named after the Ancient Greek philosopher Socrates. It is basically carrying on a friendly dialogue with two or more people, assisting them in finding answers to difficult questions by using a questioning method. You can also gauge their level of understanding about your product or service this way. People often think they know something until they are asked to articulate it. Using the Socratic Method, they must give reasoned support for their opinions, which will let you know if they have any misconceptions about what you are offering.

There may be times when your questions didn't go as smoothly as you planned. One of several things may have happened. One, you may have asked the question at the wrong time. Rushing into closing-the-sale questions before they have all the information they want, for example, can make you seem like a pushy salesperson. Two, you lose your concentration and ask the same question twice. They will most certainly think you aren't listening to them. Three, the customer may think that you are asking about something you already know or should know. You've heard that there's no such thing as a stupid question. Well, this is an example of a stupid question for a salesperson, so pay attention to what you ask.

A fourth reason questions may go wrong is because customers think you are conducting a public opinion poll by asking too many questions and not leaving enough time to answer them. Be careful not to overwhelm them. The point of asking questions is to get them to speak and elaborate on their own, not to make them feel as if they are answering a survey. A fifth possibility might be that the customers feel that a question is too personal. If it is something that you must know to complete the transaction, assure them that all information will be kept confidential. Even better, show them a written policy on how information is handled and protected. Then, if possible, let them see you putting their information in a safe place.

Lastly, never forget to let the prospect ask *you* questions. This seems so simple, yet sometimes salespeople are in a hurry to close the sale and leave before an objection comes up. The prospect should always have the opportunity to know more. People buy when they feel confident, and information gives them the confidence they need. You should also let them know that if they think of any questions in the future, you are happy to take phone calls or communicate through email and will do so in a timely manner.

Now you know *why* you should ask questions and *how* to ask questions. See the next chapter to find out *what* questions to ask.

Questions

1. Think of a time when asking questions helped you to solve a problem (not necessarily related to sales). Describe how it worked.

2. Explain how you think customers would respond to someone asking them questions versus someone giving them a sales pitch?

3. How would you respond if you were asked a question you couldn't answer?

4. Practice asking open-ended questions. What are three open-ended questions you can ask your prospects?

a)

b)

c)

5. Now think of two questions to ask prospects to gauge how they truly feel about what you are saying.

a)

b)

6.   What are three questions you can ask when you feel yourself getting upset over something the other person said?

a)

b)

c)

7.   What are three questions you can ask to determine someone's level of understanding about your product or service?

a)

b)

c)

8.   Has there ever been a time when your questions didn't go very smoothly? What do you think the problem was?

9.   How do you and your company handle sensitive information? What precautions do you take to guard it?

Answers

1. A non-threatening questioning method can be used in all arenas of life to solve problems. Hearing and asking questions makes you more open-minded allowing you to focus on solutions instead of who is right.

2. Think about how you would feel about answering questions versus hearing a sales pitch.

3. Write down what you would do if someone asked you a question you don't know the answer to. Some people would wing it. Some would try to avoid it. Some would get back to them later with the answer. Some would get them an answer on the spot. Others would just say, "I don't know."

4. Remember that open-ended questions require more than a "yes" or "no" or one-word answer. An example of an open-ended question is, "How would you feel about taking this car home today?"

5. An example would be, "How do you feel about what I've said so far?"

6. An example would be, "I'd like to understand you better. Could you please elaborate on what you just said?"

7. An example would be, "Would you please explain more? I'm not sure I understand you correctly."

8. Think of a time when questioning worked against you. Sometimes the questions are too personal, were asked too soon, are questions you already asked, etc.

9. Explain any precautions you take to protect customers' sensitive information. An example would be keeping customer records in a safe.

32 - Listen

Why do people hear only fifty percent of what you say?

Listening is an art. It seems so simple, yet many people are anything but good listeners. Studies show that we hear only about fifty percent of what is said. This is usually because we are too busy thinking about what we're going to say next instead of focusing on what other people are saying. Listening is a common courtesy, and people are drawn to people who seem to have the time and inclination to sit and listen.

When meeting with prospects and customers, eliminate all possible distractions including beepers, ringing cell phones, interruptions by assistants, music, daydreaming, eating, bubble gum chewing, the window washer dangling behind you, etc. If appropriate, take notes.

Show interest and be alert. You do this by maintaining eye contact. Your facial expressions and body language will show whether or not you are listening. Yawning is a major *faux pas*, as is looking at your watch or the clock. These will surely break rapport. Maintain your posture as well. Slouching or resting your head in your hand conveys boredom. You can also show interest by nodding or interjecting some expressions when the speaker pauses. A simple "Yes, I see," "Is that right?" or "That's so true" should be sufficient.

Concentrate on what the speaker is saying. Many people concentrate more on what they are going to say next than on what is being said. They may have social anxiety, or they just want to be prepared with a comeback. What's lost is a grasp of the facts, the ability to summarize and repeat back what was said, and the rapport that results from good communication. Never be afraid of not having something intelligent to say. At least the person won't walk away wondering if you heard a single word he or she uttered. Try to relax. It is very hard to listen effectively if you are experiencing fear or anxiety. Listening to the talker will give you something to think about to distract you from your fear.

Interrupting is also a habit of nervous people. They think if they remain quiet they'll be seen as shy, so they'll interrupt just to seem conversational. Interruption is not just a nervous habit; it is a bad-mannered habit that many people have, and that is hard to break. They may think they are helping the speaker by finishing his or her sentence, or that they have the gist of what the speaker is saying so they should get on with it by getting to the solution. However, listening patiently is more likely to pay off. Let the person finish what he or she has to say. Then, and this is important, paraphrase what he or she said to make sure you understand. This will allow him or her to confirm that you understand the problem. Ask him or her follow up questions if you are unclear. It is better to prevent misunderstandings at this stage than to try to apologize for and correct errors later on.

Listen with an open mind in order to serve your customers best. When qualifying customers (finding out their needs), be open to the idea that your products or services may not meet their needs. Refraining from pushing your products or services on people when you know that you cannot meet their needs will save time for you and the customer. You need to know what they want, how they want it, when they want it, what they are willing to pay for it, and other expectations.

Some customers cannot articulate what they want, or perhaps they don't even know what they want. Avoid trying to fill in the blanks for them, guessing what they want, or making assumptions. Instead, ask them questions and keep asking questions until you get enough information to make an informed suggestion. Silence doesn't always mean the customer agrees with you. Silence could mean the customer is confused and is too embarrassed to admit it. Or the customer may be angry but doesn't want to make a scene.

Remaining open-minded is the best approach. People resent being forced to understand. They buy from you because they feel you understand them.

Listening really pays off when dealing with an angry or upset customer. When problems arise, usually unhappy customers want to vent. Afterward, they are more reasonable and willing to work toward a solution. But before that, allow them to voice their complaint and listen calmly, intently, and in a friendly manner. Repeat their complaint back to them to show you listened and that you care.

Put aside your personal opinions. If you disagree with what is being said, you may feel tempted to interrupt them and set them straight, or at least explain your viewpoint. Most likely they won't pay attention until they've said everything they wish to say. They probably rehearsed every line of what they have to say. Just let them speak.

The bottom line is to listen, listen, and keep listening. After you think you've heard it all, ask questions and then listen some more. Don't interrupt, block out distractions, stay alert, and avoid the idea that you have to make yourself understood. People are drawn to those they feel have the time and desire to listen to them. Most of us simply want a sympathetic ear. Lend yours and you can make friends (and customers) for a lifetime.

The Sales Giant

Questions

1. What do you think your strengths are as a listener?

2. What are three things you could improve to become a better listener?

a)

b)

c)

3. How does fear or social anxiety affect the way people listen?

4. When it seems as if a customer doesn't know what he or she wants, what are three questions you can ask to help clarify?

a)

b)

c)

5. How do you react when an unsatisfied customer becomes angry? Does this help the situation or make it worse?

Answers

1. The next time someone tells you a story, stop and observe what you do well as a listener. Observe your body language including posture, arm movements, facial expressions, etc.

2. Also observe what you need to improve on, such as nervous twitches, eye contact, facial expressions, etc.

3. People with social anxiety:

   - Interrupt more

   - Concentrate on what they're going to say next instead of listening

   - Are afraid of appearing shy

   - Finish the other person's sentences

   - Are unable to paraphrase or grasp the facts

   - Don't ask as many questions or ask stupid questions

   - Ask the speaker to repeat himself or herself more often

4. An example would be – "Can you tell me more about what you are looking for to help you with your cramped car problem?"

5. Talk in general terms about how you deal with angry customers. Do they usually seem appeased and happy when they leave or does the situation end badly and unproductively?

NOTES:

33 - Put People at Ease

Why are people afraid to buy?

You think you're scared trying to make a sale? I guarantee your customers are just as afraid. They don't want to part with their money. They don't want to make a bad decision. They don't want to be trapped and tongue-tied by a slick talking salesperson.

Begin putting people at ease the moment they enter a room. You need to be confident—not the arrogant and pushy kind of confident, but an authentic, warm, and friendly confident. A genuine smile will do wonders for breaking up a tense atmosphere. Never force a smile. A fake smile can be spotted instantly and may only make the atmosphere even tenser. Smile and look interested. Let your smile and eye contact show that you welcome comments, questions, and conversation.

Etiquette will also go a long way in helping others feel at ease. It shows you are confident dealing in business situations. Manners are a basic courtesy in the business world. You will not be noticed so much for having manners, as you will for not having them. Since business etiquette is much too big a subject to cover in this book, it is recommended that you seek other sources to find out how to behave in business settings, especially in a different culture.

Humor is another excellent way to put people at ease. However, you have to be careful with humor or it can backfire on you. For example, a cynical sense of humor can be a real turnoff for someone with a very positive outlook on life. You must be able to judge whether your audience will appreciate your humor.

Introducing controversial topics should be avoided, unless you know for sure that the other person agrees with your opinions and enjoys talking about those subjects. Current events are a good catalyst for conversation, but it is always safer to avoid controversial subjects that could elicit a strong emotional response. Stick to topics like the weather, hobbies, interests, family, and work.

Making an effort to put customers at ease will no doubt increase your sales. People don't like to buy if they are scared, defensive, and suspicious. When they let their guard down, they begin to process information more receptively and make decisions more clearly. The sales pitch should not begin until a customer feels at ease.

Questions

1.   How would you handle a customer who seems uncomfortable and/or afraid?

2.   What might you be doing that causes your customers discomfort?

3.   What are some "safe," yet interesting, topics to discuss with people when you first get to know them?

Answers

1. Describe what you can do at your office to deal with people's fears. It may be as simple as offering a cup of coffee or as complicated as coaching them through their fears and anxieties.

2. Examine your own behavior. Would you be comfortable meeting someone like you? Describe any body language you use that may have an affect on people's comfort level.

3. The weather may be safe but it's not very interesting. The next presidential election may be interesting but it's not safe. Some safe and interesting topics might be your children, hobbies, sports, etc.

34 - Approaching a Prospect

What should be the first objective when you approach a customer?

You open your freezer one day. You smell rotted meat and see bright blue, green, and red guck from the popsicles that melted. You knew that old freezer would give out someday. Now you have to go buy a new one.

As soon as you enter the store, the salesperson comes rushing toward you like a defensive lineman. His hand bolts out to shake yours. Then he gives you the lowdown on several different freezers in the store. You freeze. You're being bombarded with too much information and a salesman who won't get out of your face.

If this is your idea of customer service, you have a problem. Customer service in a retail environment is much the same as it is in an office. The first goal should be to put the customer at ease. You want customers to know you are available to help them without invading their space, time, and thoughts. Any chance of helping customers to relax is often lost as soon as overzealous salespeople rush to greet them and start their sales pitch. Never ask questions as though you are a market research interviewer conducting a poll. Leave time for customers to answer your questions, and never ask more than three or four questions.

You can tell which customers are worth spending time on. If you see someone casually strolling around, never spending more than a few seconds looking at one thing before moving on, he or she is probably just looking. The customer may be killing time, admiring things he or she can't afford, or looking in advance for something he or she plans to buy in the future. You know if you approach the customer he or she will tell you, "Thanks but I'm just looking." That's fine. Let the customer just look. These customers are more likely to come back if they don't get the sales pitch when they are only casual browsers.

The customers who look at price tags, compare features, and open things to look inside, are the customers you want to focus your attention on. However, do so without them feeling as if they need to dodge you like a yellow jacket. When customers walk in, observe them for a few moments. If they seem like customers who are seriously interested in something, you can begin to walk toward them. Stop a couple feet away to avoid invading their space and say something like, "Hi, my name is _____. Are you in the market for a freezer?" If they are, go ahead and ask them more questions. If they say they are just looking, then let them know where you will be if they have any questions.

Know when to use your energy and enthusiasm on someone who is actually interested in buying. Know what to say to avoid sounding too pushy. If you receive a commission for each sale, you may be thinking you need to plunge into a sales pitch for every customer. But it isn't how hard you work; it's how smart you work. This doesn't mean you should ignore casual customers. Everyone has the potential to be a big customer. You still want to make contact with them, but use your sales energy selectively. You and your team want to avoid coming across as a brigade of sales warriors. Your customers will appreciate and remember your courtesy.

Questions

1.   Devise a plan for how you will approach customers. Answer the following four questions:

a)   What will your first words be?

b)   What will your body language be like?

c)   What will you say if the customer wants to be left alone?

2.   What will your next line be if the customer wants to accept your offer to help?

3.   Do you tend to buy more from salespeople who leave you alone to make decisions or from people who want to help you every step of the way? Explain.

4.   How do you decide whether or not to approach a customer?

Answers

1. The questions in this chapter apply more to retail sales.

a) The first words might be, "Hi, welcome to XYZ Company. Is there anything I can help you find today?"

b) Your body language will be open and relaxed. Shoulders relaxed, arms by your side, smiling.

c) "Sure, that's no problem. Please feel free to look around and if there is anything I can help you with, I'll be right over there (point to where you will be).

2. This question asks you to anticipate how customers will react to you. Being prepared is the best way to deal with unanticipated answers.

3. Each customer is different. Some will want more help than others. The most effective salespeople are those who can recognize those differences in individuals and react appropriately. A salesperson should mirror the behavior of the customer.

4. Write down your criteria for deciding if a customer is worth approaching.

35 - Make People Feel Important

What is the number one desire for most people?

Dale Carnegie told us the number one desire humans have is to feel important. Some people feel important, but they want everyone else to know that they are important. Other people doubt their importance and want some reassurance. Others don't feel important at all and crave the company of people who can give them a sense of importance. Whatever the case may be, the remedy is always to give sincere recognition and reinforcement.

You can reinforce the importance of other people in many subtle ways. You can listen patiently to a story they want to tell you. You can compliment them on an achievement. You can ask them follow up questions when they tell you about something. You can use facial expressions that show them that you are truly interested in them. Or you can say something that makes them feel as if they made a difference. Just make sure it is sincere. Obligatory flattery or politeness means nothing if you want to make a lasting impression. Think about the people you work with. If you have something exciting to tell, you never go to the co-worker who just nods and says, "That's nice." You are drawn to the people who will sit and listen, laugh, ask questions, show interest, and tell you what a great story you told.

You may be asking why you should try to make other people feel important when it is obvious that their sense of importance has led to arrogance and makes them obnoxious. Consider that the alternative is losing them as customers. They will do business with someone who recognizes and appreciates their sense of importance. If you never make them feel important, someone else will. How many customers can you afford to lose? What harm can come from making them feel important?

Start with the philosophy that everyone is important. Some people just feel it more than others. If you truly believe that everybody adds some kind of value to the world, it is easier to treat them as though they are important. Remember that people buy based on how they feel. The more important they feel, the more important your product or service will become to them.

Questions

1.   How do you feel about people you perceive to be arrogant who rattle on about all their accomplishments? How do you respond to these types of people?

2.   How can making a person feel important translate into sales?

3.   What are three specific ways you can make a customer feel important?

a)

b)

c)

Answers

1. Give an honest assessment. Arrogant people can be very obnoxious. Would you be willing to put up with one to make a sale, or is the sale not worth it to you? Discuss.

2. Think about times when salespeople made you feel important. Did it make you more inclined to buy?

3. An example would be to admire something about them like their shoes, hair style, jewelry, or car.

36 - Get the Customer Saying "Yes" Immediately

What happens when a prospect answers a question with "NO"?

Have you ever tried to convince people of your opinion and they refused to agree with anything you said? Maybe you started out with something controversial that provoked, annoyed, or offended them. Their minds shut down immediately. If this has happened to you, chances are you never managed to steer them back around to your way of thinking. You lost them before you even got started.

This can happen in sales too. You begin your sales pitch by discussing things on which your opinions differ. When people begin by answering questions with a "no" there is a physiological and psychological reaction. The mind and body are on guard for what lies ahead. They are conditioned to reject what is coming. On the other hand, when a person begins by saying "yes" the other person wants to move forward, consider new ideas, and process new information.

There is no sense in starting off on the wrong foot. Begin your sales pitch by asking questions you know will be answered with a "yes." Emphasize what you agree on and let customers know your goals are the same. Remember, you wish to accomplish the same thing they do.

One way to begin is to use the information they give you about their goals, needs, and wants and turn them into affirmative questions. For example, "So Ms. Anderson, I understand you would like to increase your sales by 20 percent by this time next year. Is that correct?" "Yes." "If I told you I have helped other companies increase their sales significantly in a short amount of time, would you be interested in hearing how?" "Yes." "Would you like me to tell you right now?" "Yes." Then tell the customer. Then ask, "Does that sound good to you?" "Yes." "Would you like me to help you in the same way?" All these yeses will put her in a frame of mind to buy your product or service.

Once people give you a "no" answer they feel as if they have to stick with what they said. Changing a "no" answer to a "yes" answer may make them think they will appear weak and wishy-washy. They may feel as if they lost the battle or appear indecisive. They may think they have allowed themselves to be coerced by a salesperson. They don't have to feel this way. They just need to get back in the mood of saying "yes." When you do encounter a "no," stop and go back to asking questions you know will get a "yes." Emphasize again that you are trying to reach the same end; you simply have a different means. Sometimes asking questions will help them forget that they originally said "no."

Get things rolling in the right direction from the very first question. Get your customers to say "yes" to your opening questions, and they'll also be saying "yes" to your closing questions.

Questions

1. Can you steer a conversation the way you want it to go or do you react to what other people say? Explain and give an example.

2. What are three questions you can ask a prospect right away that will get you a "yes" response? These questions will have to be closed-ended.

a)

b)

c)

3. What is your game plan if a customer says "no" to one of your "yes" questions?

Answers

1. Explain how effective you are in controlling a conversation. This does not mean you have power and control over another person. It merely means that you are able to direct a conversation with questions and get people to follow.

2. An example of a question that is 99% likely to get you a "yes" response is, "How would you like to save some money?"

3. You need to get the customer saying "yes" again immediately. You could either ask "Why?" or just move on to your next "yes" question.

37 - Sell Value

What is the difference between cost and value?

Price is only the fourth most important factor when it comes to buying, according to a survey of customers. Confidence in the person you are dealing with is number one, service is number two, and reliability is number three. However, for some people price is indeed the number one factor; so as a salesperson, you must address it as a priority. The problem is that people are so focused on the immediate cost that they don't think about making a wise investment for the future. Your product may cost more in the short term but it pays off in the long term. Therefore, you must convince customers that they will benefit, not just now but for days, months, or years down the road. This is called "selling the value of your product." Price is the dollar figure; cost is the value the item brings in the long term.

Successful salespeople focus on what a product or service is worth in terms of its benefits. If you just focus on price, you ignore the quality of what you offer. Most people know that they get what they pay for. Emphasizing how much cheaper you are than a competitor will only make your product or service seem inferior to what your competition offers.

If your product or service costs more than your competition, help people understand why they should pay more now in order to save money later. This is a risk to the customer because there is usually no guarantee that spending more now will pay off later. Most people are programmed to think only in immediate terms. They don't often think about anticipating or preparing for the future. Try changing their way of thinking to focus on both the present and the future.

You need to build value without lowering the price. You can build value by emphasizing a high level of service, before, during, and after the sale. Develop a reputation for excellent service and ethical, fair practices. This is a sure way to increase customers' confidence. People will pay a little more for peace of mind.

No need to do all the work yourself. Use your existing customers to sell value for you. Collect written, taped, and videotaped testimonials that describe what your product or service did for them. Then, ask them to tell their coworkers, friends, and family members about you.

Try to find out what makes customers tick. The price may be the most important ingredient in their decision, but find out what matters to them besides the price. Usually there are several factors that influence a decision to buy. If you know what those other factors are, you can begin emphasizing them to the customer. Price is a logical issue. But people are far more likely to buy something because of how it makes them feel rather than how logical the decision might be. Emotions are the primary motivating factor for making a buying decision, so place value on the emotional benefits.

Customers will place more value on your product or service if they can experience it for themselves before buying. As much as possible, allow people to see, hear, touch, smell, and taste your product or service. Give free samples, take customers for a test drive, or offer a free trial membership. This may whet their appetite just enough to make that final decision.

Zig Ziglar, renowned author on business success, explained a good way to deal with people who complain about cost. Tell them, "The price is high… but when you add the benefits of quality, subtract the disappointments of cheapness, multiply the pleasure of buying something good, and divide the cost over a period of time, the arithmetic comes out in your favor…" All you have to do is explain to customers how you provide quality, avoid cheapness, increase pleasure, and save them money in the long term. Believe in the value of what you sell and your customers will be far more easily persuaded to buy.

Questions

1. Think of something you bought that you paid more money for than you would have somewhere else. What made you buy from the more expensive place? How did you feel about your purchase?

2. How can you shift a customer's focus from price to value?

3. What are some features about your product or service you can use to emphasize value?

4. What feelings about your product or service do you want to elicit from your customers?

5. What are two ways you can allow customers to experience your product or service for themselves?

a)

b)

Answers

1. There are many reasons for why people buy from a more expensive store – customer service, warranties, guarantees, convenience, location, product quality, a feeling of security, etc. What would motivate you to buy from a more expensive store?

2. Think about all the benefits of your product or service. What will you say to persuade your customer to focus on the value rather than the price?

3. Make a list of the most important features. It may not be the features that make your products or services valuable. It may be service, in which case you should emphasize how your service differs from your competitors' (without criticizing the competition).

4. Think about how your products should make people feel. If you sell security alarms, people should feel safe. If you sell lingerie, people should feel sexy.

5. If you sell perfume, give them a free spray. If you sell a new juice, give them a free sample. Think of how people can experience your product or service before buying.

NOTES:

38 - Making the Sale

What causes most people to buy?

So far, everything in this book has been about achieving the ultimate goal of making sales. The previous chapters are tips and strategies that create an environment in which a prospect will choose you over your competitors. This chapter will focus specifically on making the actual sale. You will learn about the importance of attitude in approaching a sale, how to focus on the feelings customers experience when they buy, and how to emphasize the benefits of your product or service.

The first thing to understand is that most people buy with their emotions, not their intellect. In fact, most people buy with their emotions and then try to justify their purchases by using logic. A sports car makes people feel prestigious. A car with high safety ratings makes people feel more secure. A big truck makes people feel powerful. People usually agonize over making the most logical choice – they ask their friends, do research at the library, lie awake at night thinking about it – but in the end, they often buy something because of how it makes them feel. Making a decision, even though a customer is hesitant, will be worthwhile if there is the possibility of feeling better. Customers may think they are making a logical decision, but really they just want the security of knowing they made a good investment. They never want to have to lie awake at night worrying about losses over the long-term.

The customer has to want to buy something. Successful salespeople know how to make someone want something. Since people buy based on their emotions, experiencing the product or service as much as possible is a good way to arouse their interest. Car salespeople allow customers to take a car on a test drive. They experience the prestige, adventure, and excitement of what it's like to drive around in a fancy, red sports car. Health clubs allow a free trial membership so that prospects can feel what it's like to be on the road to weight loss and fitness. When you buy a new computer, you may get a free Internet access trial period so you can feel the joy of being connected to friends and family.

If possible, let customers use the product. This marketing strategy is devised to get people hooked on the feelings and sensations they experience when they first try the product or service. Put yourself in the shoes of a customer by imagining how you would feel if you had that product. Your knowledge of the feelings people get from certain products will help you sell that product. If you know safety is important to a car-buying mother, you can emphasize the safety features of a car that interests her. The more people can experience the product, the more attached they become to it. For a brief moment they will feel what it's like to own the product.

The way you approach a sale will also influence people. Your enthusiasm translates into their enthusiasm. A monotone voice relaying all the features of a product will do little to stir up eagerness to buy, no matter how wonderful the features are. Put some liveliness into your spiel, and they are likely to feel the same way about your product that you do. To really succeed, you have to be one hundred percent behind your product and believe that it will improve the quality of people's lives. Your passion will translate into sales.

For some people the pressure of making a good decision can be stressful. They may avoid making any decision at all for fear of making a bad one. This is where your confidence comes in. When your prospects are indecisive, they sometimes want someone to lead them to a decision. We call this hand-holding. Ask questions to find out what they need and decide on the best course of action for them. Then persuade them to take action. These are the rare customers who will appreciate your firm and decisive tone of voice and behavior. Tell them the benefits of taking the step you decided on and how those benefits will meet their needs. Don't give them too many options. This will only make them more frustrated. Make it seem as if you and the customer are making the decision together. Even better, make it seem as if the customer came up with the decision himself or herself.

What exactly is meant by "selling the benefits?" When you sell a vacuum cleaner, you don't just name all the parts inside the vacuum. Most customers won't know what you're talking about. Instead, you tell the customer it is excellent at picking up cat hair (powerful), it is lightweight (easy to maneuver), and it is compact (easy to store). The customer is left feeling as if he or she is getting a powerful machine that will make his or her life easier and more convenient. Here are some benefits to emphasize about your product. Tell them how your product or service will:

- Reduce costs.

- Increase productivity.

- Allow them to give better customer service.

- Increase morale.

- Cut waste.

- Make the job easier.

- Keep them safe.

- Make them healthier.

- Help them feel better about themselves.

- Encourage participation.

- Give them more time.

- Help them to relax.

Don't make empty comments. If you tell a customer your service will increase productivity, you better be able to tell them *how* and perhaps give examples of past achievements. Be prepared to back up your statements with facts, not opinions.

Remember that customers buy based on how they feel. Allow your customers to experience your product or service as much as possible. Emphasize the benefits, including how what you have to offer will make their lives easier, more efficient, and safer. Maintain your positive and enthusiastic attitude throughout the entire sales process, and hopefully your customers will end up sharing your enthusiasm.

Questions

1.   How can you tell what a customer feels about your product or service?

2.   What are three things about your product or service (as opposed to your competitors') that you think will benefit your customers?

a)

b)

c)

3.   How do you show your enthusiasm for your product or service?

4.   Are you able to be a leader with indecisive customers? How do you display your leadership?

5.   How would you back up these statements when speaking about your product or service?

- It will save you money --

- It will make your life easier --

- You will become more efficient --

- It will increase morale –

Answers

1. You can gauge a customer's feeling by asking them questions, watching their body language, and listening to comments they make about your product or service.

2. Think about unique features and benefits of your products or services. Make sure they are different benefits from the benefits your competitors offer.

3. Describe any behaviors that convey your enthusiasm. For example, do you smile when you speak about your product or service?

4. Being a leader in this instance means empowering customers to make a decision. This might mean giving them more information, asking questions, or even asking them to buy.

5. To get you started, one way you could back up the first statement "It will save you money" is by saying, "With this software, you will not need a cashier at this station, which means you will save a full-time salary."

39 - Product Knowledge

What is the most important reason for learning about your product or service?

When your customers ask, "How does it work?" you can either answer with authority and confidence or you can sound as if you don't know the first thing about your product. The more you know about your product or service, the more confident you can be when you speak about it. The more confident you sound, the more confident customers will be in their decision to buy from you.

You need to find out everything your customers will want to know about your product or service. Get information from the manufacturer, read it, and memorize it. Keep a cheat sheet if you have to. Anticipate questions customers may ask and prepare for them. Keep a log of questions customers ask, so you will be prepared if those questions are ever asked again.

The most important reason for learning about your product or service is to solve problems. You need to know how your customers can use your product and be able to convey this information to them. The more you know about your product and how it works, the better you can fit your product to your customers' needs.

Another reason to learn as much as you can about your product or service is to avoid giving customers correct information. Sometimes when people don't know the answer to a question they'll improvise by making up something that sounds just as good as the truth. If you don't know the answer to a question, let customers know that you will find the answer and get back to them. You will save yourself much embarrassment if you don't have to apologize later for telling them something that wasn't true.

Those of you who work in retail are in a slightly different situation. Retail salespeople should receive basic training on products, or they should know who to go to for more detailed information. Most customers will be forgiving if you are not an expert on your products, but they do expect some basic information and the ability to provide answers to their questions. If you are unable to help customers make a decision because you have no knowledge of your products, you will be giving them a reason to buy from one of your competitors.

It's simple. The more you know about your product, the more you sell. Take the time to care about what you sell and others will care too. Don't just care, be passionate about what your product or service can do for people.

Questions

1. Name a few products or services you need to know about in order to sell them.

2. Describe how you will obtain the information you need about your products or services.

3. What are some popular questions customers ask (or you expect they will ask) about your product or service?

4. How much time a week will you devote to ongoing learning?

5. How will you handle a question you can't answer? What specific phrase(s) will you use and what action will you take?

Answers

1. Make a list of what you sell.

2. Possible answers might be: to get information from supervisors, manufacturers, co-workers, in-house or off-site training, the Internet, product brochures, etc.

3. Try to anticipate what customers will want to know about your product or service. Keep a log of what they ask so you will be prepared. Some possible questions might be:

   - How does it work?

   - Is it energy-efficient?

   - What colors does it come in?

   - How will I know when it needs to be serviced?

4. The amount of time you need to spend depends on a lot of factors. It depends on what you sell, whether your product or service continually changes, how fast you learn, how effective you are at selling, etc.

5. Specific phrases might include:

   - I don't know the answer to that question, but I will find out.

   - Let me find that out and get back to you by tomorrow.

   - That would be a really good question to ask the finance manager when you meet with her tomorrow.

   - That's a very good question. I will call the manager right now and ask him.

Actions to take might include:

   - Following through and find out the answer.

   - Picking up the phone immediately and calling someone who knows.

   - Jotting down the customer's phone number and telling him or her you will call as soon as you know the answer.

   - Calling in another employee who can answer the question on the spot.

40 - Create a Presentation That Sells

What are some popular ways to make an effective sales presentation?

Now we look at exactly what takes place during a sales meeting, everything from the first impression to the closing. The more you incorporate these points into your presentation, the more likely you will be to make sales.

Make a good first impression! Tell a good joke. Fix your hair so that it doesn't look like the result of a finger in the light socket. Check to make sure there isn't a piece of broccoli stuck between your teeth. Dress so that you don't look like a character on "That 70's Show." Do a quick check on your appearance, and use a sense of humor but be careful with humor. Make sure your joke is funny to the average Joe.

Be on time! Punctuality is the first sign of reliability. Someone who is able to show up on time will be perceived as someone who can deliver when it counts.

Be enthusiastic! Exude a positive attitude and eagerness to meet people and help them. Your attitude will influence the other person's attitude about what you have to offer.

Know who your customers are! Find out where they are from, what they do, and why they want to hear your presentation. It's a good way to let your customers know you are interested in them. Plus, you will get information you may be able to use later.

Make your presentation understandable and smooth! Prepare ahead of time. You need to use language that your audience members will understand, and ask questions to determine their level of understanding. Beware of the "um" factor. Too many is a real turnoff.

Spend enough time finding out what the customer needs and wants! Spend an adequate amount of time asking questions and really listening to your customers throughout the conversation.

Match your product or service to the customer's needs! Maybe you didn't listen closely enough to his or her problem to be able to show how your product or service can solve it. As you make your case, persuade your prospect to agree with each point.

Sell benefits! Price is only the fourth most important factor in a buying decision. Customers want to know what the product will do for them. Emphasize the value of what you have to offer by stressing how it will make their lives easier, increase productivity, make their family more secure, and save them money in the long run.

Never criticize your competition! Do not emphasize what other companies cannot offer a customer. Focus on what your company *can* offer. Criticizing your competition makes you seem undignified and desperate. Pay your competitor a small compliment and then shift the focus back to what you have to offer.

Never start an argument with the customer! Refrain from arguing at all costs. It's not worth it for you or your business. If customers disagree with you, acknowledge that they may be right. If you think the disagreement results from a lack of information, gently share the information and see if the disagreement can be resolved.

Do not try to pressure the customer into buying! No need to be pushy. Usually you can tell if people are feeling pressured by reading their body language or their voice. If they move away from you, avoid eye contact, try to look distracted, look at their watch, and lose their smile, they may be trying to tell you they are not interested or they want more time for consideration.

Never exaggerate or lie! People aren't stupid. They know when something is too good to be true. Astute buyers usually know if a deal is good. They can decipher a realistic offer from a bogus or exaggerated one. Once they suspect that you are not being truthful, you will not be able to sell to them.

Handle their objections convincingly! When customers are unsure, take the time to discuss their concerns and make them feel comfortable with your answer. Never ignore their uncertainty. Never answer an objection as if it were a stupid question. Customers really need to feel confident about what you are telling them in order to feel good about their decision to buy.

Close the sale when the customer is ready! Observe the buying signals. Customers will make eye contact, ask questions specific to the product or service, make notes, and be engaging. Trying to close the sale before customers have all the information they want will make you seem pushy.

Remember to ask for the order! This seems pretty basic, yet many salespeople never even think to ask for the order. The customer might not think to offer his order, so you need to politely ask for it. Wait for the answer. If you get an objection, calmly handle it and then ask again.

Be gracious when the customer says "no!" Be sure to thank the customer for taking the time to meet with you. Often a rejection instantly changes the behavior of a person and the vibes they communicate. Handling an objection with grace makes it more likely you can come back someday and try again.

Ask to be able to help them in the future! This is one last attempt to become a partner at a later date. Perhaps customers don't need what you have to offer right now, but when they do need your service, ask that they keep you in mind.

Questions

Rate yourself on these questions asked in the chapter on a 1 to 5 scale: 5 is always, 4 is usually, 3 is sometimes, 2 is not usually, 1 is never. Then explain how you can make an improvement.

Do you make a good first impression? Rating:

Improvement:

Are you on time? Rating:

Improvement:

Are you enthusiastic? Rating:

Improvement:

Are your presentations understandable and smooth? Rating:

Improvement:

Do you spend enough time finding out what customers need and want? Rating:

Improvement:

Are you able to match your product or service to the customer's needs? Rating:

Improvement:

Do you fixate on price rather than value? Rating:

Improvement:

Do you criticize your competition? Rating:

Improvement:

Do you start arguments with customers? Rating:

Improvement:

Do you pressure customers into buying? Rating:

Improvement:

Do you exaggerate or lie? Rating:

Improvement:

Do you handle their concerns convincingly? Rating:

Improvement:

Do you ask customers to buy before they are ready? Rating:

Improvement:

Do you ask for the order? Rating:

Improvement:

Are you gracious when customers say "no"? Rating:

Improvement:

Do you ask to be able to help them in the future? Rating:

Improvement:

NOTES:

41 - Giving Your Presentation

What are the keys to a good presentation?

Giving a presentation doesn't have to be a daunting task. In fact, if you are a salesperson, you are presenting all the time. The keys to a good presentation are preparation and practice. The more presentations you give, the more comfortable you will become. This chapter provides some basic tips on how to prepare for and deliver an effective presentation.

Prepare to present. The first thing you need to do is decide on one or two objectives for your presentation. You need to do your homework before the presentation. Find out the following:

Who will attend the presentation? The content of your speech will depend on who is there.

Is attendance mandatory? If it is, you will need to be a little more engaging and entertaining. It cannot be assumed that people will be interested in what you have to say.

How much do they already know about your product or service? This is important because your audience will be bored if you are telling them something they already know.

How many people will be there? You need to know this if you have any handouts.

How will people be dressed? Dress one step up from your audience. Accessorize but never wear anything that diverts attention away from your words.

What is the layout of the room? This could be important if you intend to use visuals or move around the room to engage the audience.

What type of equipment will be available? Your visuals will be decided based on what equipment is available.

How much time is available for the presentation? Also find out if there will be time for a question and answer period.

What are the audience's needs? If possible, conduct a needs analysis before the presentation. Try to either meet with the host or talk with him or her by phone to assess the company's needs. Research the company to learn as much as you can. The more you know about the company, the easier it will be to answer their questions. Never be afraid to ask them more questions during the presentation. Every presentation should be custom-designed for each client.

Make an outline first, and then write out the whole presentation. Do not read it when you are delivering the presentation or you will sound mechanical and rigid. Start by telling your audience what you're going to tell them, then tell them, and then tell them what you told them. Your opening remarks should be only about ten percent of your presentation.

The body should be about 75 percent of your presentation. One mistake you want to avoid is overloading your audience. Sometimes the more we hear, the greater the chance your message gets lost. An overwhelmed mind will not remember anything.

Throughout your speech, keep your sentences short and use active verbs. Use words that will stir people to action. Instead of saying, "It has been said that this product helped people improve their productivity," say, "This product will improve your productivity. Here's how…" Speak to the audience directly. What will your product or service do for them? What benefits will they get? Use the words "you" and "your" frequently. Use anecdotes, stories, studies, statistics, and examples; but use terms the audience can understand. Avoid jargon, clichés, and difficult vocabulary words.

The last 15 percent of your time should be devoted to closing the presentation. Summarize what you covered and then ask the audience to take action (in the case of sales, it would be to buy). Sometimes the audience will be ready to wrap it up and leave. Keep their attention by refraining from gathering up your notes, pens, papers, and visuals. Maintain eye contact with them throughout your conclusion. Thank the audience for the invitation to speak to them. Never apologize for anything that went wrong during your presentation. Allow about ten minutes for questions and answers. Never look at your watch. Place your watch on the table in front of you if you have a tight schedule. Or you can ask the host or hostess to let you know when you have only five or ten minutes left.

If you are in a large room when you receive a question, repeat the question so that everyone can hear it. Never interrupt a person when he or she is asking a question. Make eye contact with the questioner while he or she is asking the question. Then shift your eye contact back to the audience to answer it. If you don't know the answer to a question, don't try to wing it. Just tell the questioner you don't have an answer but you will find out and get back to him or her. Never call on colleagues to answer the question unless they agreed before the presentation to serve as backup.

Visualize a successful outcome. Public speaking is the number one fear, ahead of heights, snakes and even death. Deal with fear before a presentation by staying active. Arrive early to familiarize yourself with the room and equipment. You can also spend time talking with audience members. This is a great time to find mutual interests to discuss and establish rapport. Make eye contact with interested and friendly faces in the audience. Never stare at anyone. Just look at an individual for about five to ten seconds and then move on to another friendly face. Be conscious of your breathing. Short, shallow breaths add to your fear. Breathe deeply, slowly, and rhythmically. It helps relax your body and slows down your speech.

Be conscious of nervous body language – hunched shoulders, stiff body, finger tapping, lip biting, shifting weight from leg to leg, crossing your arms over your chest, etc. In addition, mumbling, speaking too softly, talking too quickly, and interjecting "um" and "uh" repeatedly will annoy your audience. Concentrate on and correct these behaviors when you rehearse your speech. Rehearse it only three or four times. Never try to memorize it word for word. Make notes to jog your memory about key points.

Audience members will remember only about 20 percent of what they hear and 30 percent of what they see. However, studies show people remember 50 percent of what they see *and* hear. Visual aids help members of the audience retain information, focus their attention on you, and become more active in the presentation. One study by the Wharton School at the University of Pennsylvania concluded that people who use visuals were more persuasive, more professional, and had a better quality presentation. If your visuals require the use of equipment, arrive early to familiarize yourself with the equipment and make sure everything is working properly. If something goes wrong with the equipment in the middle of your presentation, briefly try to fix the problem and then go on in spite of the difficulty. It is always a good idea to have backup visuals. Maintain your composure.

Remember that you are a pro at what you do. Prepare to present by researching and asking questions. Write your speech, practice it, visualize success, and use your visuals to help you. Keep your objectives in mind and work toward those goals.

Questions

1. Assume you are presenting your product or service to an audience. What are two objectives you will focus on?

a)

b)

2. What do you need to know about the company or the individual you are presenting to in order to make an effective presentation?

3. Make a brief outline of your presentation.

I.Introduction

II.First point –

A.

B.

III.Second point –

A.

B.

IV. Third point –

A.

B.

V. Conclusion

4.   What are some verbs that will stir people to action?

5.   Briefly describe two examples of successful stories involving your product or service.

a)

b)

6.   What action will you ask the audience to take? State specifically what you will say.

7.   Are you afraid of public speaking? If so, what strategy or strategies will you use to over-come your fear?

8. Choose two possible visuals for your presentation and explain why you think they will be effective for the message you want to get across.

a)

b)

10. What is your backup plan in case your visuals don't work?

Answers

1. Decide what you want your audience to do, think, or feel after your presentation.

2. Some possibilities might be: company history, size, mission statement, goals, and a profile of the employee. If it's an individual, you might want to know if he or she is a homeowner, his or her occupation, number of children, etc.

3. Here is a sample outline for a dog breeder selling puppies:

I.   Introduction

II.   History of healthy dogs

    A.   Eyes cleared

    B.   Hips cleared

III.   Intelligence

    A.   Easily trained

    B.   Versatile – make good hunting and show dogs

IV.   Champion lines

    A.   Pedigree

    B.   Show records

V.   Conclusion

4. Three examples of action verbs are: act, decide, and pursue.

5. These would be successes that came about because of a good presentation.

6. Think about what you will say at the end. For example, if you do a presentation on knives, you could say, "There are ten of you here watching. Let's see if we can get all ten of you to take home one of these knives today."

7. What helps you to calm down?

8. Imagine which visuals would be most appropriate for your product or service. A PowerPoint presentation may be inappropriate for selling a cheeseburger.

9. An example would be overhead projectors in case your PowerPoint presentation doesn't work.

42 - Customize Your Service

Why do people crave personalized service?

There is so much competition out there, yet you think everyone should choose you. What makes you better than the rest? What do you have to offer that they don't?

The world has turned people into numbers, families into statistics, and customers into people businesses take money from. Caring, one-on-one service that treats people as individuals is appreciated now more than ever before. The more technological the world becomes, the more people crave personalized attention. The good news about technology is that it can help businesses tailor products and services to specific needs and wants.

The better you can meet and reinforce the importance of each customer's individual needs, the more likely that person is to be your long-term, loyal customer. You must acknowledge that every customer has unique needs. You can sometimes group people together, but the more effort you make to know each one individually, the more rewards you will reap. Think about it. When customers tell their friends about you, they are likely to tell a story about how they were treated. Picture them telling a story that goes something like, "I had a problem and no matter what I did I couldn't find a solution. So the salesperson found a way to solve my problem, based on what I told her about my business." People will see that you took a unique situation and came up with a unique solution that worked for that individual. On the flip side, they could have told a story about how they were going to buy from your business but you were unable to work with them to solve their problem. Now which sounds better?

Customizing service shows customers you genuinely care about them. It shows them that you get satisfaction from creating happy customers. If possible, prepare in advance to provide individualized service to your customers. This means researching their company, finding out what their needs are, and devising a proposal that best meets their needs. This will show the customer that you have taken the time to learn about them as individuals.

Never let your customers feel like they are lost in the crowd. Get to know them. Learn their names, hobbies, goals, and what their passions are. Ask if there is anything you can do for them specifically. Learn about their company. Find out what problems they face, and what you can do to help them solve their problems. People who feel that they are treated uniquely will become loyal customers and will also refer their friends to you.

Questions

1. What are three different ways you can customize your service or product?

a)

b)

c)

2. What problems might you encounter in trying to customize?

3. Has a customer ever made an unreasonable request? If so, what?

4. How did you handle the customer's unreasonable request?

5. Has a customer ever been especially pleased because you responded to his or her individual needs? Explain.

Answers

1. If you are a sales trainer, you could customize your courses based on the type of company you are contracted to train. If you run a women's health club, you could customize your membership contracts to suit the needs of working women, mothers, teenage girls, and senior citizens.

2. Customizing can be more expensive and time-consuming. Other customers may perceive customizing to be special treatment.

3. Maybe a customer asked you to do something beyond company policy, something unethical, or something that would cause you to lose a lot of money.

4. Was the way you handled it effective? If not, can you think of a better way to handle it next time?

5. Think of a time when a customer really benefited from customized service.

43 - Walk a Mile in Their Shoes

What happens to people when you can see things from their point of view?

Almost everybody likes sympathy. Snicker all you want, but it's what everyone wants and to some extent, needs. That's why we're so willing to tell our troubles to friends, family, co-workers, and even total strangers. We talk about minute health ailments, expound on our teenager's latest behavioral mischief, complain about marital relations, whine about work, and gripe about how there's never enough money. We know that strangers don't have a solution for us. Most of us consciously know that people have problems of their own. Still, we like to hear them say, "Oh, I understand," and validate how we feel about our troubles. We want their empathy and understanding.

When you can see things from other people's point of view, they open up and talk to you. Like it or not, we are not always governed by logic. Feelings play a large role in decision-making, even more so than logic. You can persuade people to do what you want them to do by showing compassion and empathy. Once they feel as if you understand and care about them, they will care about what you have to say. You don't have to be a psychologist. Just validate what they say by affirming how they feel. Tell them what you would want to hear if you poured your heart out to them.

Empathy means putting yourself in someone else's shoes and imagining how you would feel if you were that person. Even if you don't agree with the person or you think that person's concerns are petty, you can realize that he or she may have a valid reason for feeling the way he or she does. Be open-minded and non-judgmental.

How does this translate into sales and customer service? In sales, you are trying to convince customers of your point of view—that your product or service is worth buying and will be beneficial to them or their business. You can't convince a customer of your point of view until you make a genuine effort to understand it. When you consider that another person's feelings are as important as your own, you open up the lines of communication. If you hurt other people's feelings, most likely you will never convince them of your point of view. They will not be the least bit receptive to what you have to say.

Never tell people they are wrong. You can subtly and gently show them how they are wrong by presenting the facts as you understand them, but never come right out and say, "You are wrong." You will hurt their pride, embarrass them, insult their intelligence, and close down lines of communication. Even your body language and tone of voice can tell them they are wrong. Even if they are wrong, they may not think so. They may have very good reasons for believing what they do. If you can uncover these reasons, you may have the key to their motives for the decisions they make. Stay open-minded and understanding. Use the "Feel, Felt, Found" strategy. "I understand how you *feel*. Others have *felt* the same way, but we *found* that…"

When you approach customers with a proposal, think it through from their point of view before you meet with them. Ask why they should or would want to accept what you offer. What are the benefits to them? What reservations would you have if you were in their shoes? Your ability to see things from another person's point of view will be a huge asset in dealing with people and making sales.

Questions

1. Do you care about other people's troubles? Explain.

2. Are you an empathetic person? How can you show empathy to your customers?

3. Has a customer ever poured his or her heart out to you? How did you react?

4. How do you show that you understand a customer's needs?

5. If customers are wrong, how can you gently show them that they are wrong?

Answers

1. This question is really asking if you are compassionate. Do you genuinely care about other people or are you more concerned about your own problems?

2. Being empathetic means being able to identify with and understand another person's situation, feelings, and motives. Explain how you can show customers that you identify with them.

3. It can be awkward when someone pours his or her heart out. Are you comfortable in this situation or do you try to avoid it?

4. Describe any behaviors you exhibit that show you understand customers and their needs. Include telling them or repeating back to them what you understand.

5. The key here is to be gentle. People have pride. They do not like to be told they are wrong. What are some phrases you can use that both convey the message and respect the feelings of your customers.

The Sales Giant

NOTES:

44 - Handling Objections

What should you do when a customer confronts you with an objection?

Instead of thinking about customers' objections as objections, think of them as opportunities. They are opportunities to give your prospects more reasons to buy from you and to address his or her concerns. Customers are concerned about making a bad decision. They are concerned about whether or not your service can solve their problems. They are concerned about prices. When you think about objections as opportunities, you can show them that you are attentive to their concerns. You can show empathy, reassure them, and talk through their concerns. The word objection automatically conjures up images of a fight. Objections are for courtrooms. Concerns are for sales. Sometimes all customers need is a little nudge to change their concerns into a "yes" decision.

You've convinced *yourself* that your product or service is valuable, so you think your prospects will be convinced too. Maybe they will and maybe they won't. There are a myriad of reasons customers give for not wanting to buy. Listen to their concerns in their entirety, and watch facial expressions and body language to intuit what they are not saying. You may feel the urge to handle a concern with a quick rebuttal, but take time to think about it. This will show customers that you too are concerned and that you are addressing a specific concern with a unique solution. Keep your tone calm to keep a bad situation from becoming worse.

Don't get defensive, no matter what the prospect says. Take the power out of an objection by thanking the customer for bringing it up. This gives you the opportunity to learn more about your customer and what it will take to sell to him or her.

If you are unclear about the concern and need more information, ask questions. Try to find out the specifics of the customer's concern. For example, if a customer says, "This doesn't seem financially sensible for me at this time," he or she may just be objecting to the interest rate or the payment terms, not the price. A statement like that requires further probing. Sometimes he or she will tell you the truth about what they are feeling and thinking, and other times they will give you an excuse. In fact, only about 38 percent of the time will prospects give you their real reason for not buying. Usually they are afraid. If you suspect a concealed reason for not buying, be up front. After hearing their reason, ask, "Isn't there another reason you have for not wanting to make the decision to buy?" At that point, do not speak until the customer does. Sometimes this takes patience because the customer may be processing or building the courage to tell you the real reason.

Isolate his or her concerns. If your prospect seems to present one objection after another, he or she may not even know the real reason they are hesitating. For example, the customer says the price is more than he or she can afford. You should isolate the problem by saying, "I can see what you are saying about the price. Let me ask you this. If the price wasn't an issue, is everything else okay or do you have other concerns?"

Do not get into an argument with prospects under any circumstances. You may win the argument but you will lose their business. The prospect will become defensive and be turned off by anything you have to say after starting or engaging in an argument. Concerns have to be handled gently and with empathy. Customers are more likely to change their minds if they think you are there to help them as a friend, not as someone who wants to make a sale in spite of their objections. Let customers know you understand and support their concerns and then offer possible solutions.

Everything you say should be positive. If their concern is that another company offers the same product at a lower price, you may feel inclined to say that "Yes, that company's product is cheaper, but their service is terrible." Instead of telling them what another company can't offer them, emphasize what you can offer that sets you apart from your competitors. Even offering a small compliment about your competitors says a lot about you. Just make sure the compliments for your own business are bigger than the ones for your competitor.

Objections don't have to be a roadblock in your path to selling. They can actually be stepping stones – your opportunity to communicate with customers, put them at ease, solve problems, and establish long-term, trusting relationships. Listen to what customers say and don't say. Find out the real reason they are hesitating to buy. It usually stems from fear and if you can turn that fear into action, you can make the sale and keep building from there.

Questions

1. How do you feel when concerns or objections are brought up? Are you comfortable dealing with them?

2. What are three concerns about your product or service that you expect to encounter?

a)

b)

c)

3. What will you say to deal with each of these three concerns?

a)

b)

c)

4. Describe what your body language is like when you handle objections?

5. How would you handle the following statements?

- I can't really afford this –

- I don't need one of those –

- You don't have the product that fits my needs –

- I've been working with this vendor for years –

- I'd like to check out the competition first –

- I usually don't make buying decisions right away. I like to think about them first –

6. List some features about your product or service that makes you better than your competitors.

7. Who are your two main competitors and what is something complimentary you can say about each of them?

a)

b)

Answers

1. This question can measure your level of confidence. If you know your product or service well and are confident it can benefit people, then you will also feel confident handling any objection. You will even welcome them.

2. Think about what people object to. Where might your product or service fall short in comparison to the competition?

3. Write down exactly what you will say to overcome the objection. For example, if a customer complains that the horse shampoo stinks, ask the customer, "It may not smell the best, but do you know that this shampoo makes a horse's coat shiny in less than a week?" Always start your answer with, "I'm glad you brought that up."

4. Your body language should be open, concerned, and friendly. This is not a time when you want to mirror the other person's body language. You have the power to set the tone.

5. If you are selling kitchen knives, an example of how to handle the first statement ("I can't really afford this") might be: "Is cost the only concern for you or is there something else that's bothering you?"

6. Show how you are better than your competitors. This may not be a feature of your product. Perhaps you are selling the same product as a competitor. What do you have to offer that should make people want to buy from you instead of from a competitor?

7. You can be generous here, but you do not want to compliment your competitors too much. You might convince the customer that your competitors are better than you are. Even if your competitors are lousy, you must refrain from saying so. People do not like it when someone "bad mouths" their competition.

45 - Body Language

What percentage of our communication takes place using body language?

Body language is a very powerful form of communication. Body language shows our reaction to verbal and nonverbal communication. About 60% to 80% of person-to-person communication takes place through body language. In sales, you need to be aware of your own body language, and you must also know how to read the body language of your prospects and customers. If you notice a prospect crossing his or her arms and standing back, that's a clue that you need to try something else to win him or her over.

One of your first objectives is to put customers at ease. You can tell customers are relaxing when their facial expression seems soft, they smile, their posture is open, they are using hand gestures, and they nod in agreement. This chapter will give some basic descriptions of body language and how to interpret what different movements mean.

- **Eye contact**: This is probably the most important way we communicate with others. When you maintain eye contact, you show that you are interested in what other people have to say. Avoiding eye contact shows that you have something to hide or that you are lying.

- **Facial expressions**: The most important facial expression to keep in mind is a smile. A smile can change your whole attitude about a situation. It's difficult to be in a bad mood when there's a smile on your face.

- **Physical posture**: Droopy, slouching posture makes you look lazy and bored. Good posture shows you are confident and a go-getter.

- **Head position**: When your head is level you convey poise. A head that is tilted downward can convey timidity. Never tilt your head too high. That could be a sign of arrogance. To be friendly, tilt it slightly to one side.

- **Hands**: You are perceived as more open and friendly when your palms are facing up and outward. Palms facing down can be seen as aggressive. This is important when it comes to shaking hands. Make sure your hand is upright so you don't appear either dominant or submissive.

- **Handshake**: A good handshake is firm, regardless of gender, but not bone-crunching. However, adapt to the level of firmness of the other person. Do not put the other hand over the clasped hands unless you are good friends with the other person. Make eye contact when shaking hands.
  Arms: Never cross your arms, even if you are freezing and trying to stay warm. Keep your arms at your side. In some cultures the arms are sometimes clasped behind the back, but this is thought to be too formal in the United States.
  Gestures: Generally, the bigger your arm gestures the more outgoing you are. Shy people tend to keep their gestures small and their arms close to their bodies. Make your arm gestures not too big and not too small.
  Legs: Our legs tend to move around more when we are nervous, stressed, or being de-

ceptive. Rocking back and forth from one leg to another, switching leg positions, and shuffling your feet are all signs of nervousness and stress.

Physical contact: In the professional world, avoid physical contact as much as possible unless you are good friends. You might want to provide a personal touch with a pat on the back, or an extra hand over two clasped hands in a handshake, but you would be out of line. Americans especially are wary of others entering their personal space or touching them.

Proximity: Standing too close to someone can make you seem pushy or too enthusiastic. Standing too far away can make you seem tentative or withdrawn. A good sense of proximity is something we learn in childhood. About 18 inches away from someone is the norm. Note how other people react to your distance. If they back away, take that as a clue that you should move back.

Body language is especially important when interacting with people from other countries. When there are language barriers, body language becomes even more important. If you are going to meet with people from a foreign country, especially when you travel to their country, it is a very good idea to research the body language of that country. This will help you avoid any misunderstandings. Some perfectly acceptable gestures in this country, for example, are considered obscene in other countries. Save yourself embarrassment.

Be perceptive about body language. Pay attention to how others react to you. What you say may depend on what you see. Be conscious of your own body language and the message you want to send to others. Sometimes your mental approach to a situation will automatically be reflected in your body language. However, when you change your body language, you can feel more confident and speak more convincingly. Body language is one of the keys to a powerful sales presentation.

The Sales Giant

Questions

1. Explain the relationship between eye contact and self-confidence.

2. What facial expressions convey eagerness to buy?

3. Describe a good handshake.

4. Can you think of a time when you misinterpreted someone's body language? Explain.

5. What are three characteristics of your body language?

a)

b)

c)

6. What are three characteristics of your body language that you could improve on?

a)

b)

c)

Answers

1. When you look someone in the eye you convey self-confidence. Looking away means you don't want to be looked at. When you allow someone to look you in the eye, you tell him or her that you are confident.

2. When people are eager to buy, their eyes are wide open, they smile, they make various facial expressions, and the overall appearance of their face is more pleasant.

3. A good handshake:

    *   Is a firm clasp but not a death grip.

    *   Adapts to the other person's level of firmness.

    *   Has the palm facing sideways, not up or down.

    *   Involves only one hand per person unless you are good friends with the other person.

    *   Is done while maintaining eye contact and smiling.

4. This doesn't have to be confined to a sales situation. An example would be if someone stood close to you and you took that to mean he or she was interested in asking you out on a date. The truth turned out to be that he or she was from another culture and wasn't thinking about dating at all.

5. Are these characteristics that convey confidence? You might hold your hands together daintily but that doesn't necessarily mean you look confident.

6. Think of characteristics that convey a lack of confidence.

NOTES:

46 - Buying Signals

How can you tell when a prospect is ready to buy?

When making a sale, timing is everything. Asking for prospects' business before they are ready to buy could eliminate any advantage you had gained. If they say "no," you'll have a hard time getting them to say "yes" later on. Never be in a hurry. They need to have enough information about the product and feel good about you before they are ready to say "yes." You need to pay attention to the buying signals they send. These signals are transmitted both verbally and nonverbally.

Customers begin to indicate their decision to buy when they ask specific questions about a product such as, "How long does it take for delivery?" or "Can I get this in blue?" They might also ask to see informational materials again to be sure of what they want.

Customers who are nodding their head in agreement with what you are saying or are making positive comments about what you have to offer are indicating that they like what they hear. Asking for more information, especially related to cost, is another signal that they are seriously considering buying. If customers answer your questions without seeming tentative, they have decided on what they want.

Look for nonverbal buying signals as well. People who are eager to buy make more body movements. They lean forward slightly, their arms and hands are open, and their legs are uncrossed. Their faces are more expressive. Eyes are wide open, brows are unwrinkled, lips are open rather than tight, and they smile. Their bodies seem relaxed because they aren't trying to think of a way to fight you off. They use more arm and hand gestures and nod in agreement with what you are saying.

Watch for what they do as well. Reaching for and reading a sales contract, handling sales materials, looking up information on the computer, making calculations, or taking notes all mean they are figuring out how and when they can buy before they give their final answer.

These nonverbal signals, combined with the verbal signals, are strong clues that it is time to make a move. Now that you know when it is time to make your move, the next chapter will tell you how.

Questions

1.   What is your own body language like when you are ready to buy something?

2.   What will you say to a customer who shows all the buying signals but ends up saying "no" to the sale?

3.   What are three characteristics of body language that indicate an eagerness to buy?

a)

b)

c)

4.   List the characteristics of body language that indicate hesitation and resistance?

Hesitation   Resistance

Answers

1. Think about when you were eager to buy something. You probably had a little adrenaline rush. You were smiling. What else?

2. This is a time to probe the customer to find out what his or her resistance is about.

3. As mentioned above, smiling is one example. Other examples might be open body posture or relaxed shoulders. Think of some more.

4.

Resistance	Hesitation
Arms crossed	Minimal eye contact
Scowl on the face	Nervous ticks
Narrowed eyes	Not smiling but not frowning
Furrowed eyebrows	Pensive look
Closed stance	

47 - Closing the Sale

What is the one thing you have to do to close the sale?

Before you attempt to close a deal, you should have spent time establishing rapport, asking questions, sharing information, and looking for buying signals. If all these things went well, then it may be time to close the deal.

Begin with a brief summary of what you heard the customers say they need. Then briefly explain how your product or service will meet those needs. Ask customers if they agree that your solution meets their objectives. If they say "yes," then it is time to ask for their business. And yes, you have to *ask*. This may seem bold, but waiting for customers to come up with the idea on their own could waste a lot of time.

Look customers in the eye and say something like, "Why don't we go ahead with this?" or "How can I help you make the decision to buy today?" These are good ways to word your request because you are not asking a yes or no question. You are simply leading them in the right direction. Do not say anything until they answer. You don't want to redirect their train of thought.

If they say "no," ask what is holding them back. It will likely be a concern about something that has not yet been discussed. Handle the concern and then calmly ask for their business again. Keep in mind that nearly sixty percent of customers will say "no" four times before they finally say "yes." That's why the ability to handle concerns carefully and wisely is so important. It's usually not that they don't want to buy. They are just scared and you haven't reassured them enough. They want to be thoroughly convinced. This might take longer than a half hour meeting. It could take days, weeks, or even months.

There are three simple closes you can use to make more sales. The first is the "Alternative Close." This is where you give your customer a choice between two products. "Which product would suit you best, product A or product B?" It is best to keep the choice to two or three items. You have to make sure you have given your customer enough information to make a decision. When the customer answers the question, start writing up the paperwork or make a call to arrange for delivery.

The second simple close is called the "Subordinate Question Close." This is where you ask a question, which assumes that the customer is ready to buy. "I can deliver this on Tuesday or Wednesday, which would be better for you?" When the prospect answers the best day, start the paperwork. If the prospect is not ready, he or she will stop you.

The third simple closing technique is the "Assumed Consent Close." This can be a natural event and works very well if you have received agreement on every point in your presentation. "I will have to come by to measure your living room to make sure we order the right yardage. I should schedule a time for the installers right now, so that we can get the carpet in soon. As you know, we are getting very busy." If the prospect doesn't stop you from setting up the time for the installers, you will probably have the sale.

When customers do decide to buy, quit trying to sell. You don't need to say any more at this point —not until the paperwork is all done and the check is in your hands. Any additional information may cause them to change their minds. Just make small talk about conversational topics, like the weather, hobbies, etc.

Reinforce your customers' buying decision immediately. This means saying something that lets them know they made the right decision. Remind them of how your product or service will make their job easier, increase their profits, boost employee morale, or enhance their public image. Appeal to their emotions. Even a comment on increasing profit is emotional. Their supervisors will be proud of them for saving money. Customers may also have more peace of mind, or more prestige, or a good feeling that they made a smart deal with a vendor.

Another way to reinforce your customers' buying decisions is called "future pacing" your customers. Tell them how they will feel owning and using their new product. Spend time describing how your customers will use their new product. This will also be effective in reducing cancellations caused by buyer's remorse.

Make the order as easy for customers as possible. Have as much of the paperwork filled out as possible ahead of time. There is no need to allow extra time for them to change their minds. You take care of the details. You ask the questions about what color they want, how many, delivery date, etc.

A simple, but nonetheless vitally important part of closing the deal, is giving a sincere thank you for their order. Take time to thank them. Don't just glance back on your way out the door and say, "Thanks." Show genuine interest in their order by expressing sincere gratitude.

Closing can be the most exciting part of selling but only if you put some effort into it. Note the buying signals and then make your move. Summarize what the customer wants and how you can deliver it, ask for the sale, handle objections, and then ask again. Make buying easy for customers and give them a sincere thank you. The next steps are to follow through and follow up.

Questions

1.   Think of three different ways you can ask for a customer's business.

a)

b)

c)

2.   What can you do to decrease the chance of a customer changing his or her mind once he or she decides to buy?

3.   Are you someone who will keep trying after three or four "no" answers?   Why or why not?

4.   How can you avoid closing a deal before the customer is ready to close?

5.   Choose one type of closing technique mentioned in the chapter. Describe what you will say when you use that close.

Answers

1.   The three closes listed here will work, but there are many others that will also work.

2.   One thing you can do is have the paperwork all filled out so that only a signature is necessary. You could also offer lunch while filling out the paperwork. This is likely to keep the customer in your office long enough to eat so you can fill out the paperwork without the customer changing his or her mind. This is a good time to listen politely or reinforce their opinion.

3.   Think about your personality and how much you are willing and able to persevere. How does your level of perseverance affect your success?

4.   You could ask the customer something like, "Are there any more questions you'd like to ask at this point?"

5.   Using the Alternative Close you might say, "We have two different toothbrushes. One is the super deluxe, brighter-whiter toothbrush, which costs more but will remove more plaque. The other is the deluxe meaner-cleaner toothbrush, which costs less but takes more brushing to keep teeth as clean as the super deluxe would keep them. Which one suits your needs better?"

_____

_____

_____

_____

_____

_____

_____

_____

_____

_____

_____

_____

_____

_____

_____

_____

_____

_____

_____

_____

48 - When to Say No To a Sale

What should you consider in deciding to take on a client?

It may sound unthinkable but sometimes it is acceptable, even desirable, to say "no" to a sale. There are a few circumstances under which it is mutually beneficial to refuse or pull away from a sale. Financial benefit isn't always the motive. You also have to consider your goals, your time, your abilities, and your long-term relationships with customers.

Consider whether the sale goes against your goals. Sometimes a deal that doesn't seem beneficial in the short-term will actually pay off in the long-term. However, some deals have no clear benefit either way. These deals may be in direct conflict with where you want to go. If the sale doesn't seem like a good investment for your financial, career, or personal goals, then it is better to just say "no."

There may be instances in which a different company can meet the customer's needs better than you can. Perhaps the customer has a specific need, and your company provides a more general service. In this case, you can make a recommendation to the customer and ask that he or she think of you if he or she ever does need your services. The customer will be grateful and you will be perceived as a person of high integrity who looks after the needs of customers first.

Sometimes you can't deliver what a customer wants because you simply don't have time. Be honest with yourself about your time. Taking on a lighter load means you can devote more time, attention, and energy to providing the best service possible. Usually, most business is repeat business, which means you need to take care of your existing customers first. Customers who feel as if they are taken care of will return to you for more attention.

On the other hand, the customer may have all the time in the world and you don't want to wait or can't afford to wait. Customers will sometimes keep you guessing while they decide whether or not they want to buy. It may be that they'd like to buy, but they are indecisive, can't afford it, or are waiting to see if something better comes along. You can try to make them feel more confident about deciding to buy from you by offering them a money-back guarantee, a free trial, or a financial incentive for acting now. If the customer's lack of decisiveness still causes you to pull your hair out, just let the sale go. Invest your time and money in more fruitful prospects.

Lastly, you may just not like that particular customer. This isn't usually a good reason to say no, but if you have to spend a lot of time with the customer, a personality difference could wear on you and cause your level of service to suffer. It is better for him or her to have no opinion of you than to have a bad one. Unless you have taken extensive classes in theater and acting, the customer will know you do not like him or her.

Not every sale will be beneficial for you. You have to weigh the benefits against the costs. This can be tricky because sometimes the benefits are not clearly visible. A deal may not seem profitable in terms of money, but the customer might discuss business with friends at the local country club. You just never know. Consider your goals, your time, your ability to fulfill a customer's needs, the customer's willingness to buy, and your personality when evaluating the feasibility and appeal of a sale.

Questions

1.   How do you feel about saying "no" to a sale?

2.   What are three personal reasons you should say "no" to a sale?

a)

b)

c)

3.   Have you ever been in a situation where you could not meet a customer's needs? Explain.

4.   Explain how your time affects whether or not you say "yes" to a sale.

5.   How would you handle an indecisive customer?

6.   Would you say "yes" to a sale for a customer you strongly dislike? Why or why not?

Answers

1.   The answer to this question may depend on several factors. One factor that causes people to say "yes" to a sale when they want to say "no" is financial circumstance. If you are continuously prospecting, you can be more selective about which sales to pursue. Having other sales on the horizon means you don't have to accept every sale that comes along. You can focus on the sales that will be the most beneficial to you.

2.   These could be financial considerations, personality differences, time commitments, knowledge gaps, reputation, etc.

3.   Think of a time when you turned down a customer because you did not have the resources to meet his or her needs. What did you do instead?

4.   This doesn't just apply to your immediate schedule. One consideration may be that the customer will need a lot of your attention later and you don't want to make that commitment because you might not be able to fulfill it.

5.   Think of a way you can help a customer make a decision by empowering him or her. You don't want to make the decision for the customer. You need to make the customer feel that he or she made the decision. You can do this by asking questions. Give the customer two options. "Would you like it in black or white?" Asking, "What color would you like it in?" allows too many options and invites indecisiveness.

6.   Describe what it is about your personality that would make you able or unable to put up with someone you strongly dislike.

NOTES:

49 - Common Sales Mistakes

How can you turn a mistake into a success?

Benjamin Franklin got it wrong when he said nothing in this world is certain but death and taxes. He forgot one more certainty – making mistakes. They are inevitable. They are as certain as death and taxes. Everyone makes them. Why should you be any different? Becoming an accomplished salesperson doesn't happen overnight. Some people are fortunate enough to receive training. Others learn by themselves through a long, hard process of trial and error. Everyone makes mistakes.

The important thing to remember is that a mistake doesn't have to be a failure. You can turn a mistake into a success if you are able to find some way to learn from it and apply your knowledge to the next sale. This chapter will describe some of the most common mistakes salespeople make and what can be done the next time to profit from your mistake.

Failure to establish rapport. This is the most common mistake for new salespeople. Of course you are eager to make the sale, but you can't make the sale if the prospect doesn't trust you.

What to do next time. Never be in a hurry to begin your sales presentation. Spend some time getting to know customers before you launch into your presentation. They will show more interest in your product or service if you have shown interest in them personally.

Lack of preparation. When you go into a meeting with prospects you should have done some research about the prospects and the company. Appearing completely ignorant will only embarrass you. Prospects will think you don't care enough about making this sale to take a little time to learn something about them and their company.

What to do next time. Research the company using newspapers, brochures, newsletters, annual reports, and Internet web sites. Speak with the receptionist about the history of the company and any information you can obtain about the person with whom you are meeting. For a small sale the information can be brief. For a big sale, you may want to treat the information as if you are preparing for final exams.

Not spending enough time in the meeting. Running out of time or being in a hurry to get the meeting over will make the prospect feel rushed.

What to do next time. Be sure to schedule plenty of time for the meeting. Your prospects should feel as if they have enough time to get the information they need. Some salespeople feel that once the sale is final, there's no reason to stay. Remember that rapport continues to be established after the sale is made. Customers may still ask questions and need to be reassured that their decision to buy from you was the right one.

Mentioning price too soon. Price is not as important to customers as you might think. If you mention price right away, it becomes more difficult to build value.

What to do next time. What you want to do is build value first, make customers realize what your product or service is worth, and then tell them how much that value will cost. When you mention the cost first, they will think, "You'll need to give me a lot for that price." When you build value first, they will think, "I get all that and it will only cost me…"

Committing to something you can't deliver. Never be so ambitious in meeting a customer's wants that you extend yourself beyond your capabilities. Overpromising and underdelivering is a major sales *faux pas*.

What to do next time. Do just the opposite. Underpromise and overdeliver. Be honest with your customers in terms of what you can deliver. That's how you build trust.

Doing too much of everything and not enough of anything. A woman once began her own writing and editing business. The services she offered were: writing, copyediting, proofreading, researching, fact-checking, desktop publishing, and typing. Needless to say, she was so busy trying to focus on everything that she found it hard to concentrate on anything. This made her appear as if she wasn't an expert in anything, which made it hard for her to establish trust. Knowledge of your product or service is an important factor in appearing credible and trustworthy.

What to do next time. Pick what you want to do the most and make it your specialty. Choosing a specialty allows you to build in-depth knowledge of your subject area, making you sound more intelligent and reliable when speaking to prospects.

Not understanding the decision-making process. Not understanding the psychological factors involved in decision-making can lead to actions that seem abrupt, pushy, callous, or just plain stupid. Understand that buyers are often afraid. They fear that they will make a bad decision, that something better will come along in the future, or that they will somehow get burned by the seller. Beyond fear, the decision-making process was best summed up by salesman Zig Ziglar, "Customers buy when they want what you got more than they want their money."

What to do next time – Reading this book is a good step in the right direction to avoid this mistake. Do some research on how different personalities approach decision-making, how to recognize these personalities, and how to deal with them effectively.

Too much talking and not enough listening – Many salespeople feel as if they have to talk a lot to be in control. They keep talking past the point when the customer is ready to buy.

What to do next time – Give up the idea that you have to be in control. You actually have more control when you are listening. You are gathering information that will help you come up with a solution to a customer's problem. That's what sales are really about, problem-solving. Pay attention to the buying signals your customer is sending.

Failing to follow through – Following thro276ugh in this instance means doing what you say you are going to do, especially after making the sale. Before a sale is made, salespeople find themselves bending over backwards to take care of a prospect. After the sale is made, sometimes the steam is lost and the little things a customer asks for are neglected.

What to do next time – Maintain the same level of commitment after the sale that you do before the sale. Establishing a long-term relationship is the goal. Customers will notice when you forget about them.

When you are not able to make a sale, don't be afraid to ask the prospects what went wrong. Tell them you are trying to learn more about how to be successful in sales and that you want to learn from your mistakes. When they sense your sincerity they will usually be honest with you and try to help you out. Never be hard on yourself when mistakes are made. Spending too much time wallowing in your failures is unproductive and drains you of precious time and energy. Choose one or two things to learn from each mistake and move on.

Questions

1. Think of a sales mistake you made in the past. Describe it and then write down what you should have done instead.

2. How much time do you think you need for a meeting with a prospect?

3. What is a good time to mention the price of what you sell?

4. What is your specialty? Are you an expert in what you sell? If not, how could you focus your sales?

5. Do you feel that you have to be in control of a sales situation? Why or why not?

6. How can you be as consistent at working with a customer after a sale as you are before the sale?

7. Would you ever call customers and ask why you were unable to make a sale to them? What would you say?

Answers

1. Use the common sales mistakes listed in the chapter to help you think about something that may have gone wrong in the past.

2. The answer to this question will depend on how long it takes you to establish rapport, who your customer is, the nature of your business, how many questions you ask, etc.

3. Think about the product or service you sell. If you sell cars customers will want to know the price right away. If you do landscaping, you will want to convince your customer to allow you to come over and look at the yard first before mentioning a price.

4. Are your biting off more than you can chew? You can't be everything to everybody. If you become a specialist in one subject, you can carve out a niche in the market. Think about the product you know the most about or the service you are the best at.

5. This is an important question because feeling like you have to be in control will be reflected in your voice and in your behavior. People will sense that they are being controlled, which makes them resistant to listening to you. Examine your own feelings about being in control during a sales situation.

6. One way to be consistent is to keep in contact with the customer after serving him or her. This could involve making a follow up phone call, visiting the customer at his or her place of business, a birthday card, informing the customer of discount offers, etc.

7. Write a short script for what you would ask a customer, including follow up questions. The point here is not to try to make the sale again, but to gather information that will help you avoid making the same mistake in the future. You may end up establishing rapport, which could possibly lead to a sale in the future. But don't call the customer with that goal in mind.

50 - Avoid Arguments

What should you to do if you find yourself getting into an argument?

If you are a salesperson the last thing you want to do is engage prospects and customers in a verbal brawl. Avoid arguing at all costs. Your job is to diffuse a potential argument or avoid getting into one in the first place. If you win the argument, you lose the sale. If you lose the argument, you will also lose the sale. You lose either way.

If you find yourself in a disagreement with someone, the first thing to do is abandon the urge to prove yourself right or to make the other person understand you. Be the bigger person by agreeing to disagree. You may feel better, but the other person will not leave the conversation feeling good about him or herself, especially if you've proved him or her wrong in front of other people. If he or she doesn't feel good after meeting with you, how have you furthered your professional goals?

If you have a temper, learn how to control it. Count to ten, change the subject, remove yourself from the room, do whatever it takes to keep from losing control of your emotions. People are put in a very awkward position when those around them have emotional outbursts. Losing your temper in no way contributes to problem-solving. It only makes you look like a fool. It will probably lose you a few customers as well.

Sometimes people are just looking for a fight. (This will be covered in greater detail in the chapter entitled "Customers from Hell.") More often than not, people just want to be heard. They are frustrated and angry and want to let loose and you seem as good a target as any. In this case, simply listen to what they have to say. Look for areas in which you agree. Get them saying "yes" to your questions. For example, "Do we both agree that the features and condition of this car rate above average?" "Do we agree that an above average car would sell for more than the wholesale value?" This starts to turn their attention toward what you agree on, which in turn, could lead to a solution.

Even if you think the person you are arguing with is the most irrational, brain-dead creature to walk on this planet, tell him or her you will consider his or her ideas. Thank the person for his or her point of view and do it sincerely. Most people can tell when you say this simply to dismiss the discussion, so be sincere. Let the person know you find value in all viewpoints and each one is worth your consideration.

Do not act until you have had time to think. By postponing action the other person will truly believe you are considering what he or she had to say. And why shouldn't you consider it? No one is all-knowing. We learn by listening to others. We are constantly sifting through information trying to find the truth. Someone you consider your greatest opponent may have ideas worth considering. And besides, most of our so-called reasoning is actually just making arguments to continue believing what we already believe.

If you have very strong religious, political, or moral beliefs and are not able to set them aside, then you may want to consider changing your profession. Great salespeople have a common trait of being able to mirror the people they sell to. If you are constantly at odds with your customers because of an internal conflict, either find a new profession or do business with people who are more like you.

Remember, you rarely accomplish your professional goals by fighting, but you can achieve more than you expected by getting along.

Questions

1. Are you someone who feels you have to prove yourself right? Why or why not?

2. How do you act when you are angry? Does this action seem to help you in sales situations? Why or why not?

3. How do you handle someone's outburst when you are clearly not the one at fault?

4. Do you genuinely value all viewpoints? Why or why not?

Answers

1. This is really asking if you are a humble person who is able to swallow your pride. Sometimes, even though you may be right, it is really better to let the situation go. Be honest. If you are someone who has to be right, explain why you feel the need to prove yourself right. What reward do you get out of it?

2. Describe your behavior when you become angry and how it affects your professional life.

3. Describe how you react when other people treat you unfairly. Most people do not handle this kind of situation well. Are you one of them? If so, what is a better solution for dealing with people who treat you unfairly? Think of a solution that will further your long-term professional goals.

4. Most people say they value all viewpoints, but hearing them in a heated political discussion proves otherwise. Are you humble enough to take different perspectives into consideration? Give an honest evaluation of your level of tolerance for other viewpoints.

Becoming A Sales Giant

51 - Admit Your Mistakes

What will you earn by admitting a mistake?

You have made a mistake and you don't want to admit it. You know you're wrong, but what will everyone think? Should you deny it? Blame someone else? Make excuses? Insist you are perfect? You could, but it won't get you very far professionally, not in the long run.

If you are called on a mistake, do not become defensive. You may feel you need to stick up for yourself to save your pride, or your job, or your reputation; but you will earn much more respect from others if you simply admit when you are wrong. Some people just want an acknowledgment of the error and an apology. It is easier to work with people who are able to admit they are imperfect.

If you don't want to admit you're wrong, you could claim ignorance, or say you didn't understand the directions, or you were distracted. These are all cop-outs though. It's better to just admit you are wrong. Since there is no one on this green earth who hasn't made a mistake, there is nothing wrong with admitting mistakes. In fact, you may appear more human to customers. They will appreciate your humility and sincerity. If they contributed to the mistake, they may meet you halfway and admit they are partially to blame.

There is a sense of satisfaction and calmness in being able to admit when you're wrong. You never need to come up with arguments. Furthermore, admitting you are wrong moves things to the next level. When no one takes the blame, everyone is stuck in a rut trying to figure out who is guilty. Rumors fly and resentment rises. Once you can get past taking responsibility for the mistake, you are in a position to begin coming up with solutions. People will relax and say, "Okay, no problem, now what should we do?"

Moreover, many of us learn through trial and error. If we didn't make any mistakes, how would we grow professionally? See each error as an opportunity to gain new knowledge. You can reach this point only if you are willing to admit when you are wrong and choose to move on.

Questions

1. Are you someone who can admit it when you make a mistake? Explain.

2. Do you become defensive? How does this work for you?

3. How do people react when you readily admit a mistake?

4. How do they react when you never admit you're at fault?

5. Are you forgiving when others make mistakes? Explain.

Answers

1. This question is really asking how humble you are and whether you can swallow your pride. Many people are so busy judging others that they are blind to their own faults. Which kind of person are you?

2. Being defensive means you try to justify every action. You can't stand being wrong. Does being defensive further your career or hold you back? What could you gain by not being defensive?

3. People are usually less angry when someone admits a mistake. It defuses the situation and allows them to accept a solution.

4. When you don't admit you made a mistake, people get caught up in whose fault it is, why you are so incompetent, and what punishment you should receive.

5. This question is asking if you are the type of person who can let a mistake go and get on with things. Or are you the type of person who dwells on mistakes and lets them interfere with your attitude and achievement?

52 - Challenging Customers

What do "Challenging Customers" usually want?

Challenging customers are those people who go beyond communicating a routine complaint. They get in your face, scream, make a scene, and try to belittle you. Fortunately, they are few and far between, but they can seriously try your patience. They are the ultimate test of your character and of your customer service skills.

Most of the time they just want to be heard. After they've had their say, they will normally calm down so that you can move on to a solution. Lending them an empathetic ear will help calm them down. Even if you don't see their point of view, they will feel better if they see you are at least trying to understand them. A good line to use is: "I understand. I'd be angry if that happened to me too. Let's see what solution we can come up with." Normally they don't have anything against you personally. People often say a lot of irrational things in the heat of the moment. They just had a bad experience and want to make it clear to everyone so that it doesn't happen again. Many times they regret what they said after they've composed themselves.

The real test will be your ability to stay calm and act professionally. If you engage them by raising your voice and arguing back, you become virtually ineffective at working toward a solution. Do you want to win to the argument or do you want to solve the problem?

Breathe deeply and resist the urge to interrupt and reply right away. If you must speak, ask questions instead of arguing with them. Try to focus on their words, not their tone of voice. Many times we never hear what is being said because we're put off by their tone.

However, if they are swearing and insulting you, you have every right to ask them to leave. You have to take abuse and you can let them know that. Usually they will realize they are out of control and apologize.

If possible, invite the customer to meet with you in private. Sometimes they try to make a scene on purpose, thinking they can get what they want if they embarrass you enough. Inviting them to a private area can not only save you embarrassment, it can make them feel as if their complaint is important enough to be called into a manager's private work area. A safety tip: If you are in a private room do not let him or her sit between you and the door. Make sure you can get away if he or she resorts to an physical attack.

As hard as it may seem, be positive. Avoid pointing out what you *cannot* do. Reinforce what you *can* do for the customer. Offer choices if possible. This gives power back to the customer. If he or she makes a request and you feel you can agree to it, fulfill it quickly. This will calm him or her down faster.

This is not the time to deny the charges, make excuses, or blame other people. Complainers never care who made the mistake or how. In fact, an apology can go a long way in moving toward a solution. Sometimes an admission of fault is all that is necessary want to hear. Even if you are not at fault, you can tell customers that you are sorry that this happened to them. If you stand there and make excuses, you will only prolong the tantrum.

Again, remember that Customers from Hell are few and far between. Keep a positive attitude and know that these screaming, raging tyrants are rare. Approach this kind of experience as a personal challenge. Challenge yourself to stay calm. Challenge yourself to be a listener. Challenge yourself to propose solutions that satisfy everyone. And challenge yourself to stay positive in spite of these emotional outbursts. If you start to think of customers as jerks, you will begin to treat them that way—even the good ones. Maintain your perspective and you will ultimately prevail.

Questions

1. Have you ever encountered a "Customer from Hell?" Describe him or her and what happened?

2. What is it in your personality that makes you able to deal with these types of customers?

3. What is it in your personality that might need to change to make you able to deal with them more effectively?

4. Have you ever lost your temper with a customer? Describe what happened.

5. Do you have a need to win arguments? How does this affect sales and your ability to work with people?

6. What are three specific strategies you can use to calm down a shouting customer?

a)

b)

c)

7.   What are three possible solutions for unsatisfied customers?

a)

b)

c)

Answers

1. This would be a screaming, in-your-face kind of customer.

2. Describe the characteristics that help you to deal with these types of customers effectively.

3. Describe the characteristics that would keep you from dealing with them effectively.

4. What did you gain? Also describe how the customer reacted.

5. Why do you think you need to win arguments?

6. One possible strategy would be to show empathy by using phrases like, "I think I'd be pretty upset if that happened to me. Let's think of a solution to get things on the right track." Another strategy would be to speak softly. This may bring the customer's tone of voice down to match yours.

7. Probably the most popular solution is to give a refund or partial refund. You can also offer a gift certificate or free maintenance.

53 - Dealing with Complaints

What will 95% of complaining customers do if you resolve their problem on the spot?

Customers who voice a routine complaint may not be "The Customer from Hell," but they can certainly drum up some fire. The sight of a customer approaching you with the intent to complain can look too hot to handle, but it doesn't have to be. Some people think of complaints as something they have to put up with, endure, and something that takes their precious time away from their job. If this is you, you need to change the way you think about complaints.

You should welcome them. Customers who complain are merely giving you the opportunity to improve your service and show customers how well you can respond to their needs. Think about it. If you go out of your way to right a wrong, those customers will tell their friends about how well you took care of them. If you're still not convinced, 95% of complaining customers will buy from you again if you resolve their problem on the spot.

The key to dealing with customers who complain is to be empathetic. After listening to a complaint you can show empathy by saying something like, "If that happened to me I would feel the same way you do." The more empathy you can show, the more likely the customer will stay calm, allowing you to work on a solution. Most people just want to be listened to and feel as if they are understood. Always remain calm. Your mood will affect the customer's mood. You have to be in charge of setting the tone for the interaction. If you allow the customer's temperament to dictate your own, you have lost control.

The customer is always right, right? Wrong, but never say that out loud. Of course a customer can be wrong, but remember that the customers pay the bills. And what do you do when customers are wrong? You have to make them right without embarrassing them. Allow customers to preserve their dignity. How likely are people to return to a place where they were humiliated?

Assume they are innocent. Your may think they are trying to pull a fast one on you but they could also be right. They may not be explaining themselves well because they are nervous or angry. You need to find out what they are really thinking, then look for ways you can gently educate them. You have more knowledge about your product or service than they do, so it is understandable that they might be wrong. Be patient when they are having trouble understanding. It's easy for you to understand your product or service because it's your area of expertise, but could be all new information for them.

Take every complaint seriously, even if you think it's flimsy or irrational. To customers, it is an important issue. Otherwise they wouldn't bring it up. Listen attentively without interrupting and then paraphrase what the customer said to you. Get managers involved, if possible. This will show the complaining customers that you take their complaint seriously.

Never blame other people. Shifting the blame to another department or another person will only make your company look as if you are not a cohesive unit. No matter what your position, you represent the entire company. Take responsibility, even if you are not personally responsible. Think as if you are the company. Usually, customers want to hear an admission that a mistake was made. Then they are more likely to be in a frame of mind that encourages problem solving.

Think about setting up a system for dealing with complaints. Document all complaints so your employees or salespeople can learn from them and figure out how best to deal with the complaint if you get the same one again. Set goals for settling complaints. This will motivate you to think about what you need to accomplish when you get a complaint, rather than looking at it as just another chore.

Ask customers questions to find out what they want. Propose a solution and ask if that would work. If they don't like your solution, ask them what they think would be a fair solution. Most customers are reasonable if you put the ball in their court. If possible, follow up with customers a few days later to ask if they are satisfied with how things turned out. They will be pleased that you are still concerned with their interests.

The way you perceive complaints will have a significant influence on how you handle them. If complaints are bothersome to you, you will probably be brisk, annoyed, and unconcerned in dealing with customers. If you see complaints as an opportunity to improve your service, strengthen relationships, and make someone happy; you will handle them with empathy, compassion, and dignity. Take responsibility, work toward a fair and agreeable solution, and be kind. Your customers will be back to buy from you.

Questions

1.   How do you honestly feel about customer complaints?

2.   Are you able to come up with solutions that make unhappy customers happy?   Give an example.

3.   How can you help set the tone when a customer comes to complain?

4.   Do customers who complain come back to you for repeat business? If not, why do you think that is?

5.   Do you ever find yourself shifting the blame to something else?   What else could you say?

6.   What should you teach yourself and others about how to deal with complaints?

7.   Set two goals for what you want to accomplish when dealing with complaints. Focus on results.

a)

b)

Answers

1. If you really dread dealing with complaining customers, you need to adopt a new attitude. Complaining customers come with the territory. Think of a way you can approach customer complaints positively.

2. Making customers happy is often about your attitude. If you truly want to help a customer be happy, that customer is far more likely to be happy after dealing with you.

3. If you raise your voice, so will the customer. If you gesticulate wildly, so will the customer. You get the point. If you stay calm, most likely the customer will also calm down quickly.

4. Think about what you may be doing wrong. Also observe the mood customers are in when they leave after voicing a complaint. If their problem was dealt with efficiently and satisfactorily, they will generally be in a positive mood.

5. Instead of shifting the blame, you can say, "Sometimes we do make mistakes here at XYZ company. I would be happy to work with you on coming up with a solution." This would be a good thing to say if you are absolutely unable to take the blame for something you didn't do. Then you are not admitting fault, but you are not shifting the blame either.

6. People who handle customer complaints should role play how to stay calm, how to listen, how to ask questions, how to show empathy, and how to come up with solutions. They should have some specific lines to use so they know what to say or at least what kinds of words are acceptable and effective to use with a complaining customer.

7. One goal might be to have the customer come back for repeat business. Another is for customers to tell 200 of their friends and family what a great salesperson you are and how well you take care of business.

54 - Service Recovery

A customer's problem is really an opportunity to do what?

A service recovery plan is a plan that spells out how you will deal with customer when something goes wrong and your business is at fault. Your strategy and your attitude will determine whether your service recovery is a smooth operation or a complete failure. When customers come back to you because of a problem, they are giving you a second chance. This is a new opportunity to do it all over again, only better. The other option is for them to give up on you and go to a different store next time, so you should be grateful when a customer brings a problem to your attention.

Just as customers have expectations for normal transactions, they also have expectations for how problems should be solved. Customers usually don't expect you to be perfect, but they do expect you to respond to a problem in a friendly and efficient fashion. You need to devise a plan for how you will deal with possible service breakdowns.

Your plan should begin with an apology. Sometimes that alone will take care of the problem. Never blame another department or person. This will make your employees seem like a unit that lacks cohesion. Customers don't care whose fault it is. They only care that *they* have a problem. Some people think an apology is an admission of guilt, but this isn't necessarily true. An apology may just be a polite way to say things didn't work out the way they were expected to. A customer may just want an admission that a mistake was made and to know that you are empathetic to their point of view. More likely though, they want some kind of action.

The next step is to find out what action they believe is appropriate to fix the problem fairly. If it is something you can agree to, go ahead and fix the problem as quickly and thoroughly as possible. If the customer has been inconvenienced, think of a way you can make it up to him or her. Throw in a little extra. Offer a discount or, even better, offer the customer a discount on his or her next purchase. This will ensure that the customer returns to your store so you can have another opportunity to provide good service.

Don't forget that fixing the problem is only half of the recovery process. You also have to deal with the feelings of the person who was wronged. For example, a woman takes time out of her day to shop for a toy at your store. Then she gets home, puts the toy together, finds one piece missing, and her 3-year-old starts screaming because he can't play with it. Then, she has to take it apart, box it up, dig through the trash for the receipt, drive all the way back to your store, stand in line, and wait to return the item. You'd be a little ticked off too. Her time was wasted, along with a lot of effort, and on top of that she had to deal with a child throwing a tantrum because he or she couldn't play with the toy. Show empathy for customers and allow them to vent. You never know what they have been through.

Make it as easy as possible for people to get their problem resolved and be sure to communicate with them every step of the way. Customers should know who to go to in the event of a problem. They should be allowed to speak with a manager or the owner if they wish. They deserve to know why a problem occurred in the first place and about how long it will take to fix it. If the problem will take some time to fix, keep the customer informed about your progress. There's nothing more frustrating than not knowing what is going on or how long it will take. Always keep your promises when it comes to service recovery. Never put this customer on the back burner while you deal with other customers. Work overtime if you have to in order to keep your promises and fix the problem in a timely manner.

Lastly, follow up to see if the customer is satisfied. This can be an extremely effective strategy for maintaining a good relationship with your customers. It shows that you care about them and are concerned that they are dealt with fairly and efficiently.

Service recovery is all about making your customers happy. About 95% of customers will return to your business after a problem if they feel as if they were treated fairly, efficiently, and warmly. Come up with a plan for how you will deal with service recovery problems before they occur. Your attitude will most definitely be a deciding factor in whether or not customers want to give you their business in the future, so be empathetic and considerate.

Questions

1. Do you have a service recovery plan? If so, briefly explain it.

2. Do you give customers the option to tell you what action they want you to take? Why or why not?

3. What are some service recovery options that you offer?

4. How do you address the feelings people experience when a problem occurs?

5. How easy is it for your customers to get their problem solved?

Answers

1. Reminder: A service recovery plan is a plan that spells out how you will deal with customers when something goes wrong and your business is at fault.

2. Giving customers options gives them back some of the power they feel they've lost.

3. Some options might be: a refund, a partial refund, a discount on the next purchase, a gift certificate, or the item or service at no charge.

4. This question addresses your ability to show empathy. What do you do or say that shows you understand how they feel?

5. Think about your service recovery process. How much trouble would they have getting their money back? Do customers have to write a letter? Is there a complaint hotline? Do they have to stand in line for a half hour? How can you make the process easier for them?

NOTES:

55 - Following up

Following up is an opportunity to do what?

Surveys show that more than half of customers leave a vendor because they feel that the salesperson isn't concerned with them or their business. A satisfied customer is much more likely to return to your business. Most customers will not tell you they are unsatisfied. They will just chalk it up to experience and go to one of your competitors next time. How will you know if your customers are satisfied if you never ask them? Think of following up as your grand opportunity to make and keep satisfied customers. Even if they respond that they are not satisfied, this is your chance to make it right and also to keep them as a customer.

Following up with a customer can pay off in many ways. Probably the most important is that customers will know you care about them. Making a phone call or sending a personalized email or letter shows them you care enough to take a little extra time to find out how they feel about their buying experience and whether you solved their problems.

Following up can help you find out if your customers are satisfied with their products or services. Many salespeople are afraid to ask customers if they are satisfied with their purchases because they think they'll get an unpleasant response. Look at it this way. If you don't know that customers are unhappy or why they are unhappy, you can't do anything to make them happy. And a happy customer is a customer who returns to do business with you again. Unhappy customers will not only choose one of your competitors next time, they will also tell all their friends about their unhappy experience.

If customers are happy, remind them of something they did that enabled them to make such a good buying decision. This will reinforce their decision-making and lead them to believe they will make more good decisions with you and your business in the future.

Another reason for following up is to learn more about customers' needs and persuade them to come back to your store sooner than they would have otherwise. Think about car repair for example. If the customer says, "Yes, the brakes work just fine. Thank you. But I've also had this sound in the engine for a couple of months. What do you suppose that is?" Then you tell the customer to bring the car in and you'll check it. You just created more business for yourself.

Following up also allows you to make sure you have taken correct information from customers and verified exactly what they want. Send a letter the day after a meeting to thank customers for meeting with you and to verify the sale and its specifications. In addition, include information customers tell you about their needs and desires. This will prove that you were listening both to what they want now as well as what they are thinking about for the future.

Establish a schedule to remind you when to follow up with customers. You may choose to follow up within three days or three months, or even three years, depending on your type of service or product. If you sell something that needs to be replaced every so often, it is a good idea to maintain communication with your customers. If your customers indicate they buy a car about every five years, write that down and contact them just before the fifth year.

Following up is an excellent way to get referrals. After you get customers to believe you care about them, they will show they care about you too by giving you referrals. You have to ask for referrals, though. People will not think to volunteer this information. Then contact these leads as soon as you get them. Otherwise you will lose interest and start to think of a reason why you should not follow up on them.

Impress your customers by going the extra mile. Anything you can do to show customers you care will pay dividends by establishing loyalty to your company. Follow up to learn the level of your customers' satisfaction, to verify information, to correct any problems, to get referrals, and simply because you care about them.

Questions

1. Do you have a plan for following up with customers? If so, describe it.

2. What are three ways you can follow up to determine customers' level of satisfaction?

a)

b)

c)

3. What would you do if you found out that the customer wasn't satisfied?

4. If a customer is happy, what is one thing you can say to reinforce his or her buying decision?

5. Have you ever gained more business after following up? Give an example.

6. What specific phrase will you use to ask for referrals during a follow up call?

Answers

1.   Most people do not have a plan. They just follow up in special cases or whenever they feel like it. Or they follow up when they know that the customer is satisfied. A systematic plan means following up will be a part of your service philosophy.

2.   One suggestion is to visit their businesses to check in on how they are doing using your products or services. A simple phone call is the easiest way to tell your customers that you really care.

3.   Would you feel threatened by this possibility? Would you do everything you could to make the customer satisfied? Or would you settle for losing the customer?

4.   Say something like, "I'm so glad you decided to try our new carpet cleaner. Now you know what all of our other customers know – that it's more cost effective than other brands on the market."

5.   Think of a time when you received a referral or a lead by following up. Or when the customer ordered more products or services.

6.   One example would be, "I'm happy to hear that new scooter is scooting you around so well. Do you have any friends who might also like to scoot around on a scooter?"

NOTES:

56 - Feedback

What will getting feedback help you to do?

Gathering feedback can be one of the most effective tools for improving your business. You need to know what your customers are thinking about you and your product or service. Don't just listen to the positive. Negative feedback is often the more valuable because it tells you what needs to be changed. Salespeople and business owners who are in touch with how their customers think are more innovative, more responsive, and keep their customers in long-term. You need to devise a systematic way to gather feedback. This chapter will provide you with ideas for how you can get feedback and what types of questions to ask.

Conduct a survey by phone. When you conduct a phone survey, you will be asking fewer questions than you would in a written survey. People generally do not like to be bothered over the phone, so you should make it quick. Tell them it will only take about three minutes. Not five. Everybody wants five minutes of your time. Three minutes sounds more convincing. Some questions you should ask are:

- Why did you choose our company over our competitors?

- What products or services are you particularly pleased with? Which would you like to see improvements in?

- What can we do to encourage more business from you in the future?

- How can we improve our business relationship with you?

- How can we improve our products or services to help you achieve your goals?

A written survey can be more extensive. The problem with written surveys, especially those sent through the mail, is that they often get thrown away. They are less likely to be tossed if you offer an incentive, such as a gift certificate or entering the person's name in a drawing for a large prize. You should also provide them with a prepaid, self-addressed envelope. Questions to include in a mailed survey might be:

- How well did we deliver what you asked for?

- How often did we do things right the first time?

- How well did we meet deadlines?

- How quickly did we attend to you?

- How accessible were we when you needed to contact us?

- How friendly was our service?

- How well did we listen to you?

- How strong is your loyalty to our company?

- How much do you trust our company?

- How well did we meet your particular needs?

- How would you rate the appearance of our store?

- How would you rate the appearance of our employees?

- How would you rate the quality of our products or services?

- How would you rate the quality of our competitors' products or services?

- How willing would you be to recommend us?

Written surveys are more likely to be filled out if respondents can circle a response rather than write in comments. At the end of the survey, you can ask between three and five questions that require a written answer. And always leave space for additional comments. On these surveys, look for recurring answers that tell you your strengths and weaknesses.

Other ideas for gathering feedback include:

- Providing a suggestion box in your place of business, especially in places where people wait. Boredom could be the very thing that gets a pencil moving. Be sure to make pens or pencils available. Suggestions boxes should be placed out of the sight of employees to give customers some anonymity.

- Give customers a tour of your operation. This invites conversation about your processes and services.

- Listen in on customer service calls so that you can hear the complaints yourself and how they are being handled.

- Ask for feedback directly during conversations.

- Call ex-customers who have switched companies and ask why they switched and what you can do to get them back.

- Design online feedback form and advertise how to get to it.

- Send a feedback questionnaire via email. Collect business cards to get a list of email addresses.

- Include a feedback form in your company newsletter. Either provide a self-addressed, postage paid envelope or offer an incentive to get people to mail it in or drop it by your business.

- Provide financial incentives for completing feedback forms.

- Ask your employees what customers like and what they complain about.

- Consult your documentation of what customers buy and don't buy.

- Conduct a focus group session with about eight to ten customers.

Be sure to thank anyone who gives you feedback, regardless of whether it is positive or negative. Don't take criticism personally. Criticism is merely feedback that will help you improve your sales. Most importantly, show customers that you make changes based on their feedback. One way to do this is to put an ad in the paper or write a commercial that says something like, "You asked for it. Now we're going to give it to you." You want your customers to know that you listen and respond to what they want. A business that shows its willingness to change and improve will be perceived as working for the benefit of its customers.

Questions

1. Do you systematically gather feedback? If so, explain how.

2. Give examples of changes you made based on customer feedback.

3. Based on the feedback you receive, what do customers to think are your strengths?

4. Do you see any serious service gaps revealed in the feedback?

5. What are three actions you can take right now to get more feedback?

a)

b)

c)

6. How can you get your employees involved in gathering feedback?

Answers

1. Feedback needs to be systematic or it may not give you a true picture of what your customers really want. Some people ask only their best friends for feedback. You can't possibly get all points of view if you just ask the people you know.

2. These would be changes you made as a direct result of something a customer mentioned or suggested.

3. List your strengths according to customers. Are you surprised by their answers?

4. List anything your customers think you need to work on.

5. Design a mail out survey, set up a suggestion box.

6. Employees should be taught to ask questions that elicit feedback. Specific questions work best for gathering feedback. An example would be, "How do you like that new weed whacker? Are you having any problems with it that you'd like to discuss with us?"

57 - Remind Customers of Your Great Service

What happens to salespeople who remember their customers after the sale?

Your customers sign on the dotted line or carry their purchases out the door and say, "Thanks." They are pleased with your service, but a few days later they may not even remember what they bought from you, let alone that they were pleased with your service. You need to remind your customers about the great service you provide. This involves going the extra mile again with no expectation of receiving an immediate return. What you are doing is working on the next sale.

Remember your customers after a sale, and they'll remember you. Surprise them. All customers have an expectation for the kind of service they should get. Find ways to give customers more than they expect. It makes them feel as if they are important enough to receive special treatment. Salespeople who go above and beyond the call of duty get talked about because it's rare for people to go out of their way in the business world.

You may be thinking that all this "going the extra mile" will cost you a lot of money. Not necessarily. It can be as simple as making a follow up call to see if customers are pleased with their purchase, or sending a thank you note or a birthday card. Just do something that reminds people how much you care about them and their needs.

Don't be shy about tooting your own horn. If your business provides excellent service, make it known. Awards, trophies, and honors should be displayed in your front office. Write press releases to let the public know about these awards. Mention them in your advertising. Testimonials are another good way to let the world know about your great service. Use them in your advertising too. A complimentary letter by a customer can be framed and hung in your office as well. Use any means possible to remind customers you are great!

Questions

1. What are three ways to remind customers of your great service?

a)

b)

c)

2. What are two ways you can give customers more than they expect?

a)

b)

3. Describe any awards or honors you've received for your products or services?

4. What are two ways to make your honors and awards known to your customers?

Answers

1. One example is to send out a newsletter. Not only can you remind customers and prospects of your great service, you can also advertise. You can put an ad in the newspaper just to say thank you to your customers for allowing you to provide great service to them. Or you can sponsor an event and give out free items that remind customers of your service.

2. People love freebies. If you cannot afford a freebie, people will settle for some good conversation. Something as simple as leading a person to an item they cannot find instead of trying to guess which aisle it's in will give them more than they expect.

3. List them.

4. One way to make them known is to display them in your office.

58 - Thank Your Customers

How can you show customers you are truly thankful?

You probably say thank you without even thinking about it. It is instinctive, something ingrained in you from the time your mother repeated, "Say thank you," before you knew what the words meant. As you grew older, you found yourself uttering these words more as a polite way to exit a conversation than as a way to show sincere appreciation. Make a note the next time you buy something at a store. If the clerk says "thank you" does he or she make eye contact with you? Does he or she show a warm smile? Does the clerk follow up with something like, "I hope you'll come back and see us again." Is the clerk really thankful you bought something? Or, perhaps the best indication of disingenuous customer service, does he or she utter an insincere, "Have a nice day."

How can you show your customers you are truly thankful for their business? Start with your attitude. Are you truly thankful? If they weren't buying from you, would you be working? If there were no sales, would you be a salesperson? If you truly value what you do for a living, you will value your customers. They are your source of income.

Once you make up your mind to place a high value on your customers, begin going out of your way to show them how much you value them. The sale isn't over just because you sold something. It is what you do after the sale that keeps them coming back. Most business comes from repeat customers so continue to treat them like customers even after they have left the store.

You should always thank customers for doing business with you. Here are some phrases you can use after your thank-yous to make them more sincere:

- We appreciate your business.

- I hope you'll come see us again soon.

- It's customers like you that make us glad we're in business.

- Let us know how we can help you in the future.

- We're always looking for ways to improve our service. Your comments are welcome.

- I hope you enjoyed shopping here with us today.

- Is there anything else I can do for you today?

- If you need anything the next time you come in, don't hesitate to come find me.

The most effective thank-yous are immediate and specific. When you thank customers, make sure they know what you are thanking them for. This will reinforce positive behavior and show them you sincerely appreciate their actions and their feedback.

Thank customers when they compliment you or your company. We usually only hear from customers when they complain. It is rare to hear praise so make sure others know how much you appreciate their compliments. On the flip side, customers also need to be thanked for offering criticisms. If they stay silent, you won't know what your business needs to work on. Think of criticism as a gift to help you improve your business.

Thank customers when they take a recommendation from you or show they are willing to try a new product or service. Even if they don't like the product, thank them for their willingness. They will be more willing to try another product at a later time.

Thank customers when they show patience. A plain "thanks for waiting" seems hollow. Instead, you can say, "I really appreciate your patience. You now have my full attention." It carries more weight and lets them know you have shifted your focus to their needs.

People especially like to hear how they may have helped you. Always thank them when they give you a lead to a potential customer. Report back to them what happened when you followed up on their lead, even if it wasn't successful. Just let them know you listened to them and would appreciate the opportunity to contact any other leads in the future. They will want to continue helping you in the future if they know how much it means to you.

Think of ways you can go out of your way to show appreciation for your customers. A thank you note is always a nice personal touch. A discount or gift certificate would probably touch them even more. Customers who feel appreciated will show their appreciation by becoming loyal customers.

Questions

1. Pay attention when you say "thank you" and evaluate your sincerity.

2. Give an example of an insincere "thank you" versus a sincere one.

3. How can you make your "thank you" more sincere?

4. What are three phrases or questions you feel comfortable saying in addition to "thank you?"

a)

b)

c)

5. What are two other ways to thank customers when you can't do it in person?

a)

b)

Answers

1.   Do you toss out those two words like popcorn to the pigeons? Or, do you make an effort to make it sincere?

2.   An insincere thank you might be, "Thanks, have a nice day." A sincere thank you might be, "Thank you so much for stopping by today. I hope I see you again sometime soon."

3.   A thank you can be made more sincere with a smile, by changing the tone of your voice, and by saying more than just those two words.

4.   Refer to the suggestions in the chapter or come up with your own.

5.   One example would be to call them personally and thank them.

NOTES:

59 - Language of Good Customer Service

Is your use of language customer friendly?

Your language has the power to change the way people think. In sales and customer service, choose your words carefully. While several thoughtful phrases over time can establish a long-term relationship with a customer, one thoughtless phrase could instantly sever that same relationship. This chapter will give you tips on phrases that work against good customer service and phrases that can keep them coming through your doors.

Begin by changing your negative language into positive language. Words and phrases like, "can't," "won't", "didn't," "shouldn't," "not allowed," and "the policy doesn't…" conjure up images of a company that struggles, fails, and is unproductive. Drawing attention to what you cannot do for a customer makes it seem as if you aren't working for him or her. Why should he buy from you if you don't think you can solve any of his problems? It may be that you can indeed solve his problems, but your language seems to indicate otherwise. Some will argue that it is okay to use these words because you don't want to appear unrealistic, but you can be positive and realistic at the same time. Just choose your words wisely to convey uncertainties.

My favorite negative line is when you ask someone for something and they say, "no problem." I'm sure they mean this in a positive way. This is so commonly used yet it is so wrong. Why would you want to bring a problem into our conversation or business relationship? When someone asks me to do something and I am willing to do it, I almost always say, "My pleasure." Say both phrases out loud right now. "No problem, my pleasure." Which statement sounds more positive?

The next advice is to align yourself with the company. When dealing with customer complaints, avoid saying, "The policy doesn't allow that" or "Management won't let us…" People use these phrases as a way to get them off the hook, but to the customer *you* are the company. You make the company look bad when you try to shift the blame. Even though you are not personally responsible for a policy, speak as though you are the company, offering what you can do for the customer, and then move on.

Personalize your service by using the word "I" instead of "we" or "they." Customers want to know you are personally involved with the company. If you are the one dealing with a customer at any given time, you *are* the company. Case in point: some companies insist that the word "I" be used in personal correspondence. Would you rather receive a letter that says, "I would like to thank you for coming to visit Peacock Industries" and is signed by an individual, or would you rather read "The company would like to thank you for your visit" signed by Peacock Industries? Most people like the personal touch.

Let's think of some phrases that would make you turn around and walk out a door. The first is, "I don't know," and leave it there. The customer's first thought is, "Well then, why do you work here?" A better phrase would be, "I'm not sure and let me find the answer for you," or "Let me ask someone who can find out." You may even want to say "I don't know but…"

Another phrase that can raise the customer's temperature a notch is, "That's not my department." Customers don't care which department belongs to whom. They just want an answer. Use the same phrases as above. No need to say, "That's not my department's responsibility but…" Just let them know you are on a mission to get their question answered.

"You'll have to…" Do customers have to jump through hoops of fire to make a purchase from you? Whatever it is they have to do, can you do it for them instead? Customers hate being sent on wild goose chases. They hate having to take several steps to accomplish something that should be easy. In their minds, you should be grateful for their business so why should they have to do so much work to help you out? Make it as easy as possible for them.

"We can't do that." If you can't, you had better have a good reason. Again, try to avoid telling customers what you can't do and emphasize what you *can* do. If your customer wants a cash refund and you only offer exchanges, instead of saying, "We can't give you cash back," say "We can exchange your merchandise for other merchandise."

Similarly, try to avoid the word "no," especially at the beginning of a sentence. If a customer asks you a yes or no question such as, "Can you give me a cash refund?" you can avoid saying no by answering, "For returned merchandise we can offer you an exchange." Then the customer is more likely to think about what is offered rather than what is denied.

The term "no problem" seems innocent enough. However, why bring the word "problem" into it at all? There's no sense in making customers think you are turning a potential problem into a non-problem. Alternative phrases might be: "I'd be happy to," or "I would be pleased to take care of that for you," or "Sure, let me help you with that" or "It would be my pleasure."

"Can I help you?" Of course you can but how? If you can't help them then you probably shouldn't work there. A better phrase would be, "*May* I help you?"

"I'll get to you in a minute." This phrase makes it sound like you're going to take him outside and pummel him. Something less abrasive might be, "I'll be with you in a moment" or "After I help this customer, I'll be right there to help you."

"Are we done?" This sounds callous, like you are trying to get this person out of the way so you can get on with what you were doing before the customer interrupted you. A better closing would be, "Is there anything else I can do for you today?"

Think about the phrases you use and how you think a customer reacts to them. How would you react to your own phrases if a salesperson used them on you? If you are a manager, try an exercise in which your employees jot down the phrases they use and have them come up with alternative phrases they believe are more customer friendly. Have them share these phrases in a group setting so your business can come up with the best possible phrases to improve customer service.

Now think about some messages you may be sending both in what you say and how you act. Sometimes you might be saying one thing and communicating something entirely different with your body language. "Sure, I can do that for you," while rolling your eyes does little to convey your eagerness to help customers. Customers want you to care about serving them. They want to know you enjoy your job. How many times have you been through a checkout line at a supermarket and asked the cashier how her day was going and she looked at her watch and said, "Only two hours to go...?" Wouldn't you rather hear her say, "I am doing great. I get to meet a lot of interesting people while I check groceries." People who make work seem like work are not fun to do business with.

Customers can sense when someone doesn't like them or doesn't want to be bothered with them. One-word answers to their questions, lack of eye contact, and an unsmiling face are all signs that an employee doesn't want to be bothered. Likewise, avoiding customers by carrying on a conversation with co-workers, talking on the phone, working at the computer, and generally avoiding a customer's attempt to get your attention tells customers you would rather be focused on your own tasks rather than on the needs of your customers.

Lastly, customers can sense when your mouth tells them they are right, but your body language tells them they are wrong. A dispute is left unresolved and the customer is made to feel uncomfortable. Give customers the benefit of the doubt. Is it really worth arguing over? Isn't your job to make sure the customer is pleased and not to win a personal battle?

Earlier it was mentioned that you should use the word "I" instead of "we" or "they." Customers love a personal touch. However, in a different context the words "you" and "yours" are just as powerful. "I" is good for establishing rapport and handling conflicts, but "you" helps you make a sale. It shifts the focus from what you want to what your product or service can do for another person. When people hear "you" and "yours" they perk up, listen more, and become receptive. They feel like they are going to get something good.

When making a sales pitch, use forward thinking terms, "right now," "of course," "for sure," and "will do." Words like "maybe," "perhaps," "possibly," and "might be able to" plant doubt in the buyer's mind. They want to be enthusiastic about their choice and you can help instill that enthusiasm.

Never use your Harvard education on a non-ivy league audience. This means to use simple words. You will not be so convincing about your product if no one can understand what you are saying about it. Also, avoid slang terms. Slang is too casual and some terms are used only within certain cultural groups. You will probably only embarrass yourself. Likewise, the use of profanity will do nothing to endear you to others. Never make yourself look cheap by using profanity.

Some people buy into the merits of political correctness, while others get chills up their spine just hearing those two words. Regardless of how you feel about being politically correct, one cannot deny that language impacts the way customers think about you and whether they choose to buy. This is not a discussion on the virtues of political correctness, but there are potentially dangerous phrases and words that should be avoided in a professional setting.

You may think calling your customers "honey" or "sweetie" is innocent enough. After all, you're a nice, old man with grandchildren. You don't mean any harm by it. It's just your way. No one should take offense to something like that. Now look at it from the perspective of a customer who is a successful thirty-old woman. To her, it is patronizing and disrespectful. It goes against everything her parents, friends, teachers, and experience have taught her about communicating with people. It is being too intimate and too familiar. She may feel demeaned, like you are putting her down because she is a woman. It doesn't matter if you think she is being overly sensitive. In the end, it only matters how she feels about you and your service. Basic courtesy and respect mean something different for each person. Stay on the safe side by using words that show respect.

Hopefully, reading this chapter has left you thinking about the language you use. You have to stop and think about how your words may affect other people. Pay attention to how other people's language affects you too. When someone says something that makes you feel good, adopt those words into your own language. You have to retrain your mind, and maybe even slow it down, to choose your words more carefully. Attitude affects language too. A positive attitude will be reflected in positive words. A professional attitude will help you avoid profanity, patronizing words, sarcastic humor, and negative phrases. Choose the right words and your customers will choose you.

Questions

1. What are three features of your language usage that you could improve?

a)

b)

c)

2. Pay attention to the language you use when dealing with customers for one day at work. Jot down some phrases you used that would seem to conjure up a negative image of your company. List them here.

3. Now rewrite those negative phrases as positive ones.

4. Discus how your body language relates to what you say.

5. Describe the level of sophistication of your language. Address word complexity, slang, profanity, industry jargon, and culturally or politically sensitive words.

Answers

1. Think about profanity, bad grammar, street jargon, talking above people, and other issues raised in this chapter.

2. Are you surprised at what you say?

3. Practice using the positive phrases at work tomorrow.

4. One example would be telling a customer how happy you are to meet him or her while looking away. Your words and body language do not match and the customer becomes skeptical about your sincerity.

5. Verbal sophistication can help or harm your relationship with customers. If your grammar is that of a fifth grader you will turn off a lot of educated people. However, if you sound like a Rhodes Scholar from Oxford, you may put off people with less education. It all depends on your audience. Make sure that your language is appropriate for your profession.

NOTES:

60 - Customer Service by Phone

What do customers do when they are on the phone with you?

"If the phone would just stop ringing, I could get some work done." All of us have thought this at one time or another. Unfortunately, this frustration will transfer over to your use of the phone and how you interact with the customers who call. The phone should not be thought of as a distraction to your business. More likely than not, it breathes life into your business. Many of the most successful people in business view the phone as a huge liability. It can cause a lot of harm and damage to your business if not used properly.

The phone may be the only contact customers have with your business, so a good first impression is crucial. Customers form a mental image of you and your company based on the service they receive by phone. This can include anything from the tone of your voice, the amount of time they are put on hold, and the number of buttons they had to push to reach a live human being.

A live human answering the phone is always recommended over an automated telephone system. The following are some tips for great customer service by phone.

- **Answer the phone promptly:** The phone should never ring more than 3 times. If it does, have a trained backup person to answer the phone.

- **Greet the caller:** Greet the caller courteously and identify yourself. Never just say "Flea Enterprises." Say "Thank you for calling Flea Enterprises. This is Judy speaking."

- **Articulation and volume:** Enunciate and make your voice easy to hear without being too loud. There is no need to bellow out a greeting.

- **Tone of voice:** The tone of your voice should be pleasant and cheery. Even if this caller is the thirty-fifth person to call with the same question, never make it sound like he or she is just another annoying call.

- **Smile:** Smile when you speak on the phone. Your smile will translate into a friendly tone of voice. You cannot be grumpy when you are smiling.

- **Speed of speaking:** Do not talk too fast or too slow.

- **Pronouncing names:** Customers should be referred to by their names. If possible, keep notes in your customer files about pronunciation.

- **Identifying a customer:** Customer files should be looked up when the customer calls. You should make notes to remind yourself what they called about and what you discussed with them.

- **Working with a computer:** If you need to use a computer while on the phone with a customer (to look up or record information), describe to the customer what you are doing. Telling customers what you are doing on the computer lets them know what is going on. Never criticize the speed of your computer, or lack of it. They will think your company, like your computer, is antiquated and unreliable.

- **Taking notes:** Take notes to add to the customer's file. The notes will also help you resolve any problems.

- **Focus on the caller:** Avoid any distractions, especially from other people. Carrying on two conversations at the same time is rude.

- **Train employees:** Train your employees on how to answer the phone. They should be knowledgeable about how to greet customers as well as about company policies and procedures. It is frustrating to hear, "I'm not sure who would be in charge of that." Employees should know whom to transfer the call to in order to answer a question.

- **Create cheat sheets:** You should have one cheat sheet for transferring callers to the appropriate person and another for frequently asked questions you receive by phone.

- **Transferring a call:** When transferring a call, stay on the line until the transfer is complete. This will prevent callers from having to call back if they are lost during the transfer. If you know that the person asked for is not in, ask the caller if he or she would like to leave a voice message before automatically transferring their call to voice mail. Some people prefer to leave a message with a person.

- **Putting callers on hold:** Avoid the hold button as much as possible. Always ask permission before putting people on hold. If it seems as if they've been on hold for a while, ask if they would like to continue holding or if you should take a message.

- **Calling back:** Never ask customers to call back if the person they want to speak with is not in. If they volunteer to call back, fine, but don't ask them to. Take a message instead. If you have too many calls to handle at one time, it is okay to take their name and number and call them back. Make sure you call back within a reasonable time – 10 to 15 minutes.

- **Taking messages:** Messages should be complete and accurate. Always get the phone number where the caller can be reached. You might have this on file, but it is easier for the person receiving the message if he or she doesn't have to look it up. The date and time are also important. Make sure that your name is on the message so that the recipient knows who to go to if they have any questions.

- **Returning messages:** Return message quickly, the same day if possible.

- **Closing the conversation:** When closing the conversation, ask the caller something like, "Is there anything else I can do for you today?"

- **Listen for what is not said:** Sometimes customers say that nothing is wrong, but their tone indicates otherwise.

Some companies find it necessary to use an automated telephone system because of financial constraints. For many people, these systems are a maze of never-ending frustration. You can ease the discomfort by making your system as user-friendly as possible.

Never force users to listen to a long speech before they get to the selections. Short and to-the-point messages are the best. Use short words and plain English and offer Spanish if necessary.

Keep your menus simple and unambiguous. The choices should be clear and kept to a maximum of five. Users get confused and forgetful if you have more than five options. More than two levels of choices makes callers feel as if they are wasting too much time pushing buttons and listening to menus. Let users know where they are. For example, "You have selected 'technical support'."

The ability to access a live human being is paramount to the perception of good service. If none of the options fit their needs or they are unable to understand the menu, customers may just decide to abandon your company for a more user-friendly company. Furthermore, there are still rotary phones out there. You can keep from losing a customer by providing the option to press "0" or stay on the line to speak with an operator.

When users select an option, often what follows is dead silence. The first thing they may be thinking is; "Did the transfer work?" "Should I press the number again?" "Did I get disconnected? "Should I hang up and do it all over again?" Playing music or a "thank you for holding" message while on hold can ease these fears.

Employees and salespeople should understand that for many customers phone service is valued as much as face-to-face service. Make sure your telephone service is prompt, courteous, friendly, and as easy to use as possible. If you treat your telephone calls the same way you do your in-person customer service, you will succeed in retaining happy customers.

Questions

1.   What are three of your phone strengths?

a)

b)

c)

2.   What are three of your phone weaknesses?

a)

b)

c)

3.   How many times should the phone ring before you answer it?

4.   What is a good way to greet a customer when you answer?

5.   What do you think will be different if you smile while you are on the phone?

6.   When you are using a computer to help customers, what is a good way to let them know what you are doing?

7.   What are five main points about phone service that you would teach employees?

a)

b)

c)

d)

e)

Answers

1. Think about your greeting, articulation, volume, tone of voice, body language, technical skills, focus, etc. Take advice from co-workers. You may think your biggest asset is a friendly tone, but perhaps your co-workers will tell you your friendly tone sounds like baby talk.

2. Same as above.

3. A maximum of three times.

4. Write exactly what you will say when you answer the phone. For example, "Good morning. Flea Market Enterprises. This is Sandy speaking."

5. Smiling will put you in a upbeat mood.

6. Tell the customer what you are doing about once every eight to ten seconds.

7. Assume that employees will remember only three or five of the tips you give them.

NOTES:

61 - Customer Service by Email

How should you compose an email?

Email is the best thing to come along since sliced bread. However, you could stick a knife in your relationship with your customers if you don't use email with some etiquette. The most basic thing to remember is to compose an email the same way you would a written letter. This chapter outlines some basic tips for communicating effectively via the Internet.

- **Salutation:** Just as you would write "Dear Mr. or Ms." in a letter, do the same thing with email. It is baffling that people never feel the need to address the recipient of an email. Personalize the message by acknowledging the person to whom you are writing.

- **Be specific:** Be as specific as possible in addressing your message. "Dear User" and "Dear Customer" don't have quite the same ring as "Dear Ms. Parker."

- **Subject line:** The subject line should also be as specific as possible. Usually, when we can't think of a good subject line, we just type "Hello." This is *not* a good business subject line. "Financial report for August meeting" is a better subject line, for example.

- **Watch your grammar:** It is safe to say that more attention is paid to grammar in written letters than it is in emails. Show that you care about your email communication by capitalizing, punctuating, and spell-checking. It is unprofessional to write emails as though you are a teenager chatting with friends.

- **Watch your humor:** Never treat customers like old friends unless they are. You never know what kind of humor they possess, so don't try to be funny.

- **Formality:** On the other hand, never be so formal that your emails. Personalize your emails are dull. It is okay to compliment the recipients or address them by their names, but never try to be cute.

- **Impulsive email:** Never ever send off an email when you are angry. If you are angry, you can write an email, but send it to yourself first and then come back to it the next day. You'll be surprised how much you've calmed down.

- **Gestures and voice inflection:** Even if you are not angry but want to make a point, be careful about how you might come across to people who can't see you. You might think you are being polite, but the inability of the recipient to see your gestures and hear your voice could mean you come across as condescending or harsh. The best thing to do in this case is have another person read your email before you send it. Also keep in mind that people who send you messages may not be as wise as you are about gestures and inflection. Give them the benefit of the doubt if their emails seem haughty. Most likely, that is not their intention. If you use ALL CAPS it indicates that you are shouting at your recipient.

- **Ditch the smiley faces:** Smiley faces are for kids and for Wal-Mart. Communicate like an adult by using words. The same goes for email abbreviations. Assume your reader does not know that IMHO means "In My Humble Opinion."

- **Relevant text:** When responding to a message, include only relevant text. Cut everything else out or make sure it is at the bottom of the email so recipients don't have to scroll through pages of type to find out what they said about the subject at hand.

- **Sign off:** Every email should have both a greeting and a sign off. It shows the recipient that you are done speaking and that you wish to say goodbye. Yes, recipients know it's from you by looking at your email address, but they also can tell who a written letter is from by the return address and yet letters always finish with "Sincerely" or a similar sign off. Do the same for your email.

Remember that email is only one tool to communicate with customers and business associates. Never become so reliant on email that you ignore other communication methods. Some people may think email is too impersonal, especially if you are trying to build rapport before or after making a sale. Others may prefer email. Just don't become so lax with your email that you come across as unprofessional. The bottom line is to treat email communication the same way that you treat a written letter.

As a salesperson you should also know that it is about ten times easier to ignore an email. It is much more effective to see someone in person, especially if the stakes are high.

One last word on email – when customers take the time to write you, they should receive a response in a timely manner. Every email should receive a response within 24 hours, preferably the same working day. At the very least, acknowledge receiving the message and indicate by what date you will address the problem.

These tips will set you on the path to excellent email customer service. Your attention to the details will pay off and speak volumes for your company's image.

Questions

1. Do you treat email communication the same way you treat written communication? Why or why not?

2. Describe why you use email in your business? Does it replace face-to-face or written communication for you?

3. What are three traits about your emails that you know you need to change?

a)

b)

c)

4. How can you prevent sending an email you will later regret?

5. Have you ever sent an email you thought was funny but it backfired? Explain.

Answers

1. If you answer no, what is your justification for being so lax with email?

2. Describe the purposes of email at your business. One purpose might be to get important communication out quickly. Another might be to provide a short cut for answering customers' questions. Another might be just because everybody else is, and you don't want to appear archaic.

3. Use the information in the chapter to answer this. A couple of examples might be: including a salutation and ditching the smiley faces.

4. Have someone proofread it or hold off sending it for a day or two.

5. A good way to prevent this is to get a second opinion, preferably from someone who doesn't have the same sense of humor.

NOTES:

62 - Managing Employees

Employees treat customer based on what?

You might be wondering why a chapter on management is in near the end of a book on sales. Here's why – employees who feel good about themselves at work will pass on those good feelings to your customers. This chapter is about how to get the most out of your employees. How employees treat customers is a direct reflection of how management treats employees. If you treat your employees with compassion and understanding, that is how they will treat your customers.

Hiring the right employees is the first ingredient of good customer service. If you have to train your employees to be nice, they probably shouldn't have been hired in the first place. It is amazing the number of employers who never check an applicant's references and talk with their previous supervisors. It isn't hard to call up a supervisor and ask if the employee is a friendly and upbeat person. You want to hire people who are naturally pleasant and have a positive outlook on life. This doesn't just apply to front counter employees. Why not hire friendly and positive people for the entire organization? Even if their skills don't match up to other applicants, wouldn't you rather train positive people to perform jobs than to train experienced people to be friendly?

Once you hire good employees, make them part of your overall customer service plan. Involve them in the planning, implementation, and evaluation of your goals for customer service. Let them know they play a central role and that they will be rewarded for success. It is crucial to involve them in planning so that they will feel like part of the team rather than like subordinates having orders handed down to them. Employees become excited about an organization's goals when plans are made in an atmosphere of teamwork.

Positive motivation comes from having direction. Managers and employees should get together and set specific service goals for the company. They can set smaller goals for each employee. Goals give people a sense of purpose. They feel like they are moving forward toward achieving some end, rather than aimlessly going through the motions. All goals and expectations should be in writing and posted for everyone to see as a constant reminder.

The goals should be measurable. People pay attention to what gets measured at regular intervals. Once a year is not often enough. Employees will slack off eleven months of the year and then step it up a notch the month before being evaluated. Bi-monthly or quarterly evaluations are even more effective.

The positive results of those evaluations should be rewarded. Good service is often taken for granted. Set up a reward system so that the better the service, the bigger the reward. Customers should play a role in evaluating service performance. Devise a way to get customer feedback, like surveys, suggestions boxes, or even evaluation forms. Possible rewards might include:

- A bonus added to the employee's paycheck

- Coupons or gift certificates

- Extra vacation time

- A project employees particularly enjoy

- Promotions

- A more flexible work schedule

- Autonomy – freedom from supervision

- Raffles

- Free lunch or dinner

- Tickets to sports events

- Company products or services

Customer service doesn't have to be face-to-face. Don't forget to reward your employees who work behind the scenes in ways that directly relate to good customer service. Sometimes employees will make an extra effort to get something done on time, to make something easier for a customer, or to solve a problem. Let them know that being thoughtful and working hard are appreciated.

Foster open communication with employees. Ask them about their knowledge of customers. They work on the front line so they should know better than anyone. Ask what customers are saying. Ask what they are worried about. Your employees can be your best ally in meeting customers' needs and wants. Never punish employees for telling you what they think. This only discourages them from taking the risk to communicate with you again. When you get a good idea from an employee, put it into practice, and let everyone know whose idea it was. Make employees look good. They will love the recognition, and it will encourage more employees to solve problems and think creatively.

If you must criticize employees, never do it in public. The point is not to humiliate them, but to change their behavior. Being overly critical will only alienate employees, resulting in a resentful and tense working atmosphere.

Some tips for criticism seem in order. Gone are the days of authoritarian leadership. Great leaders today lead by respecting a person's dignity, handling people gently, and treating them more like colleagues than subordinates. Humble yourself first before doling out criticism. Employees will feel as if you relate to them in some way and that you have made the same mistakes they make. They will see you as someone teaching from experience instead of from a power trip. Let them know that no one is immune to mistakes, and that life (including your job), is a learning experience.

When you must criticize an employee's behavior tell him or her a few things he or she does well first. Never cancel out those good things with the word "but" at the end. Change "but" to "and". An example of what not to say: "You handled that transaction very efficiently, but next time be more patient when a customer wants to explain his or her situation." A better way to say it would be: "You handled that transaction very efficiently, and the next time a customer wants to explain his or her situation, maybe he or she will be able to find a patient salesperson. Do you think customers would appreciate that?" This is a more subtle way of letting employees know that they need to be more patient. Ending with a question also gives employees the opportunity and power to evaluate what they did and what they can do differently next time. People are more likely to see and admit their mistakes if they are handled gently and diplomatically. When people are criticized, they feel the need to be defensive and justify their actions. A wall goes up and learning generally stops.

Customer service is not just a one-day, once a year training program that gets people motivated for about two weeks until next year's training rolls around. Good customer service has to be ingrained in your employees' minds. Regular reminders at staff meetings, one-on-one spontaneous training sessions, articles in company newsletters, whatever it takes—make customer service the number one component of your business culture. Show employees that it is a priority by providing extensive training, setting service goals, and rewarding employees for positive customer service. Happy employees make for happy customers.

Questions

1. Quickly summarize your management philosophy.

2. Now summarize what your management style is really like.

3. Give some examples of how your employees treat your customers based on how you treat your employees.

4. When you call job applicants' references, what questions do you ask them?

5. How do you involve employees in planning, implementing, and evaluating your goals for customer service?

6. How do you facilitate a team atmosphere?

7. How do you give employees a sense of purpose in their jobs?

8. How do you reward employees for good service?

9. Describe your style of communication and how your style helps or hinders achieving company goals.

10. Describe how you criticize employees. How do you think they feel when you give them negative feedback?

11. How can you become a better leader?

Answers

1. Describe your underlying values as someone who manages people. This is not about your style. It is about your beliefs. For example, don't say, "I am fair." Say something like, "I believe that managers should be humble enough to do everything that they require their employees to do."

2. Now describe your style. Does your actual style match your philosophy? Or do you preach but not practice?

3. Look for direct correlations. For example, if you say things that embarrass your employees, do they say things to your customers that embarrass them?

4. Make a list of questions you should ask an applicant's references. These questions should apply to both their personality and their work habits. Also ask about how they get along with co-workers and how they treat customers. Don't just ask, "Are they customer service oriented?" That is too broad and a closed-ended question. A better question would be, "What are three things the applicant does well when interacting with customers?" In order to do this, the applicant has to sign an authorization to release information, which you may have to fax the former employer.

5. Describe how employees play a part in customer service other than standing on the front lines?

6. A team atmosphere has to be actively facilitated. If you let employees create their own teams, you will get cliques and animosities. Managing people means managing conflicts.

7. Employees need to feel that their individual roles make a difference. They also need to feel personal job satisfaction.

8. There are hundreds of ways to reward employees. You can ask them what they want or you can surprise them. You can also let employees know who has received rewards and why as a way to motivate them.

9. In addition to answering this question, critique your style. Is it effective? What do you need to improve to be a better communicator?

10. Consider the tone of your voice, your words, the length of the criticism, whether you say anything positive, and the opportunity for employees to ask questions.

11. Critique your overall style of leadership. Sometimes the best way to find out what kind of leader you are is to give employees an anonymous evaluation form. Employees usually give honest and fair evaluations of their supervisors. Try it sometime and be open to what they say. You should also study leadership styles.

NOTES:

Conclusion

Now you know what it takes to be great! A passion for sales is what makes great salespeople Sales Giants.

"You don't have to be great to get started, but you do have to get started to be great," writes Les Brown, a successful entrepreneur, motivational speaker and author.

Motivation is the key factor. You can tell the difference between people who have a passion for sales and people who should be in another line of work. Those who love sales don't have to drag themselves out of bed in the morning. They don't get tired of listening to people's problems. They don't give up when their plan doesn't work.

People with a passion for sales love other people. They love to ask questions and listen. They love to solve problems. They seek opportunities to improve their skills and build their knowledge. They are motivated enough to overcome fears, deal with failures, and try new approaches.

Think how successful you want to be one year from now. Every decision you are confronted with in the meantime will either help or hinder you from achieving your goals. Break it down in terms of day-to-day business. If you decide to cancel an appointment with a client so that you can sleep in, you are making a decision that keeps you from being successful that day. If you pull yourself out of bed and put on a happy face, even though you didn't get much sleep the night before, you are making the decision to be successful that day.

Every choice you make will determine your level of success. Most people would agree that achieving "greatness" doesn't happen overnight, yet many people are willing to let a day go by without doing anything that contributes to their long-term goal. Each day must be looked at as an opportunity for becoming just a little bit better. Eventually, all those days of small successes will add up, and you will be the great salesperson you set out to be.

This may be the concluding chapter, but there really is no conclusion to learning about sales. It is a never-ending process. It is your willingness and enthusiasm that led you to buy this book, read it, and complete the questions at the end of each chapter. It is that same willingness and enthusiasm for learning, that "burning desire to be great," that can make you a successful salesperson.

I wish you success in everything you do!

Tom Monson

NOTES:

Bibliography

Bettger, Frank. *How I Raised Myself From Failure to Success in Selling*. New York: Simon & Schuster, 1983.

Canfield, *Jack The Success Principles*.

Carnegie, Dale and Associates, Inc. *The Leader in You: How to Win Friends, Influence People and Succeed in a Changing World*. New York: Pocket Books, 1993.

Farber, Barry. *Superstar Sales Secrets*. Franklin Lakes, NJ: Career Press, 2003.

Farber, Barry. *The 12 Clichés of Selling and Why They Work*. New York: Workman Publishing, 2001.

Girard, Joe with Robert Casemore. *How to Sell Yourself*. New York: Warner Books, 2003.

Girard, Joe with Stanley H. Brown. *How to Sell Anything to Anybody*. New York: Warner Books, 1977.

Hopkins, Tom. *How to Master the Art of Selling*. New York: Warner Books, 1982.

LeBoeuf, Michael. *How to Win Customers & Keep Them For Life*. New York: Berkley Books, 2000.

Pinskey, Raleigh. *101 Ways to Promote Yourself: Tricks of the Trade For Taking Charge of Your Own Success by Visibility Marketing Expert*. New York: Avon Books, 1997.

Robins, Tony. *Awaken The Giant Within*. Simon and Schuster, New York, 1991

Waitley, Denis. *The New Dynamics of Goal Setting*. New York: William Morrow and Company, Inc., 1996.

Westerfield, Jude. *Giving a Presentation* (Barnes & Noble Basics Series). New York: Silver Lining Books, 2003.

Zemke, Ron. *Delivering Knock Your Socks Off Service* (Third Edition). New York: AMACOM, 2002.

Zigler, Zig. *See You at the Top*. Gretna, LA: Pelican Publishing Company, 1982.

Zunin, Leonard and Natalie Zunin. Contact: The First Four Minutes. New York: Ballantine Books, 1972.

NOTES:

NOTES: